JEWS UNDER TSARS AND COMMUNISTS

T0028248

Russian Shorts

Russian Shorts is a series of thought-provoking books published in a slim format. The Shorts books examine key concepts, personalities, and moments in Russian historical and cultural studies, encompassing its vast diversity from the origins of the Kievan state to Putin's Russia. Each book is intended for a broad range of readers, covers a side of Russian history and culture that has not been well-understood, and is meant to stimulate conversation.

Willard Sunderland, Henry R. Winkler Professor of Modern History, University of Cincinnati, USA

Published Titles

Pussy Riot: Speaking Punk to Power, Eliot Borenstein
Memory Politics and the Russian Civil War: Reds Versus Whites,
Marlene Laruelle and Margarita Karnysheva
Russian Utopia: A Century of Revolutionary Possibilities,
Mark Steinberg
Racism in Modern Russia, Eugene M. Avrutin
Meanwhile, In Russia: Russian Memes and Viral Video Culture,
Eliot Borenstein
Ayn Rand and the Russian Intelligentsia, Derek Offord
The Multiethnic Soviet Union and its Demise, Brigid O'Keeffe
Nuclear Russia, Paul Josephson
The History of Birobidzhan, Gennady Estraikh
The Afterlife of the 'Soviet Man': Rethinking Homo Sovieticus,
Gulnaz Sharafutdinova
Why We (Still) Need Russian Literature, Angela Brintlinger
Russian Food since 1800: Empire at Table, Catriona Kelly

Upcoming Titles

*Russia's History Painters: Vasily Surikov, Viktor Vasnetsov, and the
Remaking of the Past*, Stephen M. Norris
A Social History of the Russian Army, Roger R. Reese
A Territorial History of Russia, Paul Werth
Black Encounters with the Soviet Union, Maxim Matusevich
Gulag Fiction from Stalin to Putin, Polly Jones
The Invention of Russian Time, Andreas Scholne
The Tolstoy Marriage, Ani Kokobobo

JEWS UNDER TSARS AND COMMUNISTS

THE FOUR QUESTIONS

Robert Weinberg

BLOOMSBURY ACADEMIC
LONDON • NEW YORK • OXFORD • NEW DELHI • SYDNEY

BLOOMSBURY ACADEMIC
Bloomsbury Publishing Plc
50 Bedford Square, London, WC1B 3DP, UK
1385 Broadway, New York, NY 10018, USA
29 Earlsfort Terrace, Dublin 2, Ireland

BLOOMSBURY, BLOOMSBURY ACADEMIC and the Diana logo are trademarks of
Bloomsbury Publishing Plc

First published in Great Britain 2024
Copyright © Robert Weinberg, 2024

Cover image: 'RUSSIAN CIVIL WAR propaganda poster issued by White Army
shows Trotsky as red devil (© Pictorial Press Ltd / Alamy Stock Photo)'

A catalogue record for this book is available from the British Library.

A catalog record for this book is available from the Library of Congress.

ISBN: HB: 978-1-3501-2916-0
PB: 978-1-3501-2915-3
ePDF: 978-1-3501-2917-7
eBook: 978-1-3501-2918-4

Typeset by Newgen KnowledgeWorks Pvt. Ltd., Chennai, India
Printed and bound in Great Britain

To find out more about our authors and books visit www.bloomsbury.com
and sign up for our newsletters.

CONTENTS

ILLUSTRATIONS

Maps

TIMELINE

1762–96: Reign of Catherine the Great

1772, 1793, and 1795: Partitions of Polish-Lithuanian Commonwealth by Russia, Prussia, and Austria that led to the incorporation of Jews as subjects of the Russian monarchy

1835: Official establishment of Pale of Settlement

1861: Emancipation of serfs

March 1881: Assassination of Tsar Alexander II (ruled 1855–81) and outbreak of pogroms

October 1905: Tsar Nicholas II (ruled 1894–1917) issues the October Manifesto granting civil liberties; outbreak of pogroms

September–October 1911: Trial of Mendel Beilis

July 1914: Outbreak of the First World War

February 1917: Abdication of Tsar Nicholas II and end of Romanov dynasty

March 1917: End of Pale of Settlement

October 1917: Seizure of power by Bolshevik Party and establishment of communist regime

January 1924: Death of Vladimir Lenin

1928–32: First Five-Year Plan that marked the beginning of the planned economy, rapid industrialization, and collectivization

June 1941: Germany invades Soviet Union

May 1945: End of war between Germany and Soviet Union

May 1948: Establishment of State of Israel

March 1953: Death of Joseph Stalin

1985: Mikhail Gorbachev initiates policies of *glasnost'* and *perestroika*

December 1991: End of Soviet Union

March 2000: Election of Vladimir Putin as president of Russian Federation

ACKNOWLEDGMENTS

I am indebted to Gene Avrutin, Zelda Bank, Carolyn Dean, Philip Decker, Nirav Mehta, Bob Moeller, Steve Norris, Rakhmiel Peltz, Molly Petchenik, and Francesca Trivellato for their incisive comments and suggestions on various drafts of this book. I also want to thank the Provost's Office of Swarthmore College for providing funds to defray the costs of reproducing many of the images. In addition, Darya Herman of The Bridge Research Network deserves my thanks for providing high-resolution images from *Bezbozhnik u stanka*, *Veche*, and other publications.

My largest debt of gratitude goes to Laurie Bernstein who has shared her life selflessly with me for over forty year and who has devoted countless hours to reading and editing every essay, book, and review I have written. She has polished my prose, fixed grammatical and syntactical errors, and helped me organize my ideas and clarify my arguments. I do not exaggerate when I write that she deserves all the credit for the strengths of this book, while its shortcomings are due to my pigheadedness not to heed her advice.

INTRODUCTION

The drawing entitled The Miraculous Flower (Figure 0.1) appeared in the March 22, 1907, issue of *Veche* (The Realm), a right-wing, antisemitic newspaper published in Moscow for several years in the early twentieth century. It offers a stark and unequivocal pictorial depiction of the debate about the status and treatment of Jews (known as the Jewish question) in the Russian Empire and illuminates some of the constituent parts of the Jewish question as it was articulated prior to 1914. The drawing is a commentary on how the campaign by Jews in the empire to acquire civil liberties and political freedom would backfire in the aftermath of the Revolution of 1905, when Tsar Nicholas II sanctioned elections to a legislative assembly and legalized political parties.

In the first panel a plant with two leaves emblazoned with the words "The Jewish Question" begins to sprout. The caption reads, "On the fetid soil of the liberation movement, a mysterious plant began to grow." In the next panel two male Jews with stereotypical large hooked noses and sidelocks use watering cans labeled "bribes" and "the press" to tend to the plant, which responds positively to the care and attention. As the caption ironically notes, "The benefactors of the human race diligently looked after the flower and gave it various beneficial fertilizers." Panel three shows the plant with a new leaf called "freedom," along with a stem and a flower already beginning to bloom and labeled "equal rights." The Russian word for "freedom" is *svoboda*, but it is rendered here as *shvaboda*, with a sibilant "s." The misspelling and mispronunciation of the word mimicked the purported speech impediment that supposedly prevented Jews from speaking proper Russian.[1]

In the next panel other Jews come to admire the green thumb of the two Jews; the caption reads, "The Kikes waited from day to day for the flower to bloom. Finally, the bud cracked open." But the flower scares

Figure 0.1 The Miraculous Flower

Veche (The Realm), no. 33 (March 22, 1907). Courtesy of the Bridge Research Network

off the Jews, who run away because the stems of the fully blooming flower are giving the *mano in fico*, an insulting and dismissive hand gesture in which the thumb is placed between the index and middle fingers. The *mano in fico* enjoyed common currency in the early twentieth century and expressed indignation, the equivalent of thumbing one's nose at someone or telling someone to "get lost." In this context, however, it was an obscene gesture, like showing someone the middle finger.

In 1897 Jews made up approximately 4 percent of the Russian Empire's total population and comprised the largest group of Jews that ever existed. Why did this relatively small minority group of slightly more than five million assume such an outsized place in the political calculations of both tsars and communists? Why did Russians and their leaders believe that the presence of Jews was a menace to the social, political, and economic order, and thereby merit the scrutiny of and regulation by government officials? What was the specific nature of Jewish society that purportedly posed an existential threat to the interests and stability of tsarist and communist societies?

In the words of one historian, the nineteenth century was "the age of questions," a time rife with discussions of problems concerning politics, nationalism, gender, class, ethnicity, religion, and culture.[2] The presence of Jews in Europe generated myriad questions and figured prominently in inquiries about the well-being and integrity of European society and culture. *Jews under Tsars and Communists: The Four Questions* focuses on the "Jewish question" (*evreiskii vopros* in Russian) in tsarist Russia and the Soviet Union, where discussion of the subject took on heightened importance.[3] Of all the questions that occupied Europeans' attention, it was the Jewish question that was the most persistent, virulent, and strident. This book examines popular and government attitudes in Russia over the course of the nineteenth and twentieth centuries that viewed Jews as a problem that had to be addressed through state policies. The fact that successive governments over the course of two centuries viewed Jews as a problem underscores the belief that Jews threatened the welfare of non-Jews and could never be integrated into mainstream society. Examination of the Jewish question found its way onto the pages of books, pamphlets, newspapers, and journals, and it became the focus of numerous government commissions and reports.

Since *Jews under Tsars and Communists* draws upon materials produced by persons who identified as Russians and wrote in the Russian language, I use "Russian" and "Russia" as a matter of terminological convenience, as a catchall geographical phrase that encompasses non-Jewish (or Gentile), Slavic subjects of the tsar such as Ukrainians, Belarusians, and Poles. Distinctions rooted in language, culture, religion, and place of residence existed among the various Slavic peoples populating the empire, but the content of the Jewish question remained consistent among the Gentiles who lived in tsarist Russia. Eliding these differences does not alter the ways the Jewish question was posed and debated. I also use the terms "Russian Jews" and "Russian Jewry" when referring to the period of tsarist rule (which ended in 1917) and "Soviet Jews" and "Soviet Jewry" when discussing the era of communist rule (1917–91).

The book exposes the reader to some of the contours of the Jewish experience under tsars and communists, but its primary purpose is to uncover the underlying motivations for framing the presence of Jews in tsarist Russia as a problem that required a solution. While not all subjects of the tsar harbored prejudices against Jews, the Jewish question loomed large in the minds of a broad cross-section of people living in the Russian Empire, despite the fact that the vast majority of non-Jews never even crossed paths with a Jew.

The Jewish question came in myriad forms, but all its manifestations shared a common characteristic: Jews were seen as an alien group of people who did not fit into mainstream society and were intent on oppressing and exploiting non-Jews through control of the economy, particularly commerce, industry, banking, and finance. Jews were accused of nefarious business practices and taking advantage of non-Jews by manipulating the market and lending money at high rates. As we shall see, a fundamental characteristic of the Jewish question remained consistent over time, namely that certain aspects of Jewish life and society jeopardized the non-Jewish community. The Jewish question encompassed more than economics; it touched upon all aspects of Jewish life, from culture and religion to politics and affairs of state. Indeed, the terms of the question remained pretty much unchanged. Prior to and after 1917 the tsarist and communist governments regarded the Jewish religion, and Jews themselves, as a danger to mainstream culture, unwilling and unable to fit into the world of their non-Jewish neighbors. They worried not only that Jews were exploiting non-Jews, but also that Jews were politically unreliable and subversive. How could the Jews, the authorities thought, be relied on to be loyal and patriotic subjects? Essentially, Jews fell victim to deep-seated prejudices that tagged them as insular, clannish, and inimical to all things non-Jewish.

Since late antiquity the Jewish question existed wherever Jews lived. For over two millennia the persistence of the Jewish question had been expressed in similar terms: host societies tolerated the presence of Jews, whom they viewed as an alien and dangerous minority whose insular customs, religious beliefs, and way of life challenged the integrity of society. Since the Middle Ages, for example, Christians believed Jews took advantage of non-Jews, elevating the collective self-interest of Jews above that of Gentiles. They regarded Jews as unscrupulous, crass materialists who, as shopkeepers, money-lenders, and financiers, took economic advantage of vulnerable Gentiles: Shakespeare's Shylock in *The Merchant of Venice* embodies European society's prejudices toward Jews. Non-Jews believed that Jews were incapable of fitting into mainstream society and perceived them as a degenerate people who corrupted all persons with whom they had contact. The Jews, it was maintained, intended to subvert the existing social and political order and dominate non-Jews. The very values and tenets of Judaism were believed to be the source of the Jews' hostility toward non-Jews, not to mention Jewish efforts to exploit their gentile neighbors.[4]

The Jewish question had special significance in the Russian Empire, which was home to the largest number of Jews in all of Europe: some 45 percent of European Jewry lived in tsarist Russia on the eve of the First World War. In the Russian Empire, where no one enjoyed full civil liberties and political freedom at the turn of the twentieth century, Jews continued to endure discrimination at the hands of tsarist officials, and they became integrated into the Russian world at a much slower pace than Jews in other European countries, thereby keeping alive the Jewish question, which was more expansive, broadly conceived, and debated.

Emancipation and Citizenship

The Jewish question was expressed in similar terms throughout Western and Central Europe when, beginning in the seventeenth century, governments and their officials, intellectuals, and political activists debated whether or not Jews merited emancipation. The term did not refer to the granting of personal freedom to Jews, who, while being second-class subjects, were not enslaved. Rather, it touched upon the issue of whether legal equality should be extended to Europe's Jews, and disabilities, such as special taxes and exclusion from certain professions, should be lifted.[5] The granting of legal equality and civil and political rights to Jews occurred in the context of emerging nation-states proclaiming that political sovereignty resided in the body of citizens who comprised the nation. The rise of the liberal nation-state facilitated the acceptance of Jews as full and equal citizens, and Jewish emancipation entailed efforts to promote the acculturation and integration of Europe's Jews into society. Governments and societies in Central and Western Europe, the United States, and Canada grew more tolerant of Jews with the rise of political liberalism, civil society, and the nation-state from the 1800s onward. In those societies where legal and political equality became the norm, the Jewish question was less important because rights of citizenship pertained, in principle, to everyone, Jews and non-Jews alike. Still, the Jewish question existed and generated heated discussions in the arenas of politics and culture, particularly because emancipation was not a straightforward process and was characterized by many bumps along the way. The gains of emancipation were fragile and subject to reversal.[6]

Whether or not Jews deserved equal standing as members of the nation was a hotly contested subject, and the debate revolved around those characteristics of Jewish religious, cultural, and socioeconomic life that, it was believed, prevented Jews from fitting into gentile society. What, if anything, did Jews have to do in order to demonstrate that they were worthy of equal treatment before the law? What did Jews have to do in order to undo centuries of misgiving, lack of trust, and suspicion on the part of the Christians in whose midst they lived? In some countries, like France after 1790–1, Jewish men received full rights of citizenship as a matter of the political principles of the French Revolution. In other places, emancipation came in fits and starts, as in Prussia and the Austro-Hungarian Empire. By the start of the twentieth century, Jews in Great Britain and throughout most of Western and Central Europe enjoyed equal legal and political status with non-Jews. But regardless of the country, extensive debates framed the emancipation process. They focused on those elements of Jewish life that set Jews apart from their host societies and hindered their being more like Gentiles. According to those officials and intellectuals who set the terms of the debate and helped formulate government policies, in order for Jews to enjoy the benefits and privileges of citizenship, they needed to jettison certain aspects of their lives that distinguished them from the people among whom they lived. Rather than speak Yiddish, Jews needed to learn French, English, or German. Rather than dress distinctively, Jews needed to blend in more by adopting the dress and lifestyle of the French, English, or German. Jewish males, including young boys, had to forgo wearing black caftans and pants, white shirts, and yarmulkes (religious skull caps), beards, and sidelocks, while married Jewish women had to stop wearing wigs and covering their arms, legs, and head in public. Even Jewish boys from observant families dressed in traditional garb as evidenced in Figure 0.2 taken in the 1920s.

Rather than sending their children to schools that focused only on the teachings of Judaism, Jews needed to study subjects that would enable them to participate in secular endeavors. Rather than relying on commerce, finance, and shopkeeping to earn a living, Jews needed to alter their socioeconomic profile by engaging in what were viewed as productive labor such as agriculture and handicraft production. Although Jews were not expected to forsake their religion, some Gentiles hoped that the end result of emancipation would be conversion to Christianity. In short, nothing about Jews should distinguish them from non-Jews except their religion, which nevertheless remained an object of suspicion and distrust and in need of reform. But as we shall see, the debate in Russia involved more than a discussion of whether Jews could and should integrate and acculturate into gentile society: at the heart of the matter lay the belief that Jews resisted doing so for nefarious reasons.

Jews in Tsarist Russia

Even though this book is not a history of Jews in the Russian Empire and Soviet Union, some background information is critical to understanding the formulation of the Jewish question.[7] The emancipation of Jews in the Russian Empire would have to wait

Figure 0.2 Two boys in traditional garb, 1920s

Photo Archive, Jerusalem. 3393_14

until all subjects of the tsar enjoyed the rights of citizenship that prevailed in many European states by the end of the nineteenth century. Tsarist Russia had a long way to go before it acknowledged and institutionalized liberal political values. Nonetheless, the Jewish question that emerged in the Russian Empire hewed closely to the debate found elsewhere in Europe, focusing on the Jews' religious, cultural, and socioeconomic characteristics that distinguished them from the world of non-Jews with whom they lived. While the ultimate disposition of the Jewish question would occur at some future date, Russian Jewry found itself the subject of public discussion and government policies designed to understand, regulate, and influence Jewish society. The same prescriptions that marked the Jewish question in Western and Central Europe also took place in the land of the tsars: Jews should learn Russian; Jews should dress and look like Gentiles; Jews should engage in work similar to that performed by non-Jews; Jews should learn secular subjects; and, finally, Jews should rid their life of what many Gentiles considered fanatical and barbaric practices, such as circumcision and kosher butchering.

Until the 1770s Jews were banned from residing in the Russian Empire. Tsar Ivan IV expelled Jews in the mid-sixteenth century, and in the 1740s Empress Elizabeth prohibited Jews from residing, even temporarily, in the empire. All that changed several decades later, when Russia, along with Prussia and Austria, dismantled the Polish-Lithuanian Commonwealth in a series of partitions in 1772, 1793, and 1795. As a result, hundreds of thousands of Jews found themselves living as subjects of Catherine the Great; a century later slightly over five million Jews—known as Ashkenazi Jews—lived in the Russian Empire. Nearly all resided in the westernmost regions of the empire, the territory that stretched from the Baltic Sea in the north to the Black Sea in the south and comprises today's Ukraine, Belarus, and Lithuania. Under 1 percent of the Jews living in the Russian Empire called the Caucasus and Central Asia home, regions where they had resided for centuries.[8] Until the late 1800s Jews in European Russia shared, for the most part, a common language (Yiddish) and culture that was intimately linked to the rhythms of daily life determined by observance of Judaism. As we shall see, Jews in the Russian

Empire experienced significant changes as a result of new economic opportunities, urbanization, industrialization, and secularization and the erosion of traditional religious values and behaviors that had taken root in the fifty or so years prior to the outbreak of the First World War in 1914.

The tsarist government had to contend with people from many ethnic, cultural, and religious backgrounds, many of whom fell under imperial control as Russia expanded to the southeast and east and acquired territories in Siberia, Central Asia, and the Caucasus from the seventeenth century onward. Like the Jews, these new imperial subjects (many of whom were Muslim), along with Poles and members of other ethno-religious groups who lived in the former Polish-Lithuanian Commonwealth, were not Orthodox Christians. Even though these non-Jewish subjects were frequently subject to autocratic policies designed to Russify them, they did not command the kind of attention paid by those government officials tasked with developing policies toward Jews. The fact that millions of adherents of Catholicism, which tsarist administrators viewed with deep suspicion, did not raise the same concern among tsarist officials was presumably due to the shared religious beliefs of Orthodox Christians and Catholics, though the government was suspicious of the latter group's allegiance to the Pope.

We can trace the emergence of the Jewish question in Russia to the final decades of the eighteenth century and the early nineteenth century.[9] The first issue that officials had to address concerned the legal status of those Jews now living under tsarist authority. Where did Jews fit into the complex legal and social system of the empire? Until 1917 Russian society was divided into corporate estates (*sosloviia*, plural; *soslovie*, singular), which categorized all subjects of the crown and imposed legally binding rights, responsibilities, and obligations. Given the fact that Jews tended to engage in trade, shopkeeping, and business of some kind, we should expect the tsarist bureaucracy to have integrated them into the merchant *soslovie*. Instead, they decided to categorize them as "town dwellers," even though many resided in the vast rural hinterland.

Catherine the Great decided to limit Jewish residence to territory that would become known as the Pale of Settlement. As shown in

Map 0.1 Pale of Settlement

Courtesy of Bill Nelson Maps

Map 0.1, the Pale comprised the westernmost regions of the Russian Empire (primarily Ukraine, Belarus, Lithuania, and eastern Poland) that had been home to Jews for centuries prior to the incorporation of these territories into the Russian Empire. The Pale also encompassed territory near the Black Sea, which had been ceded to Russia by the Ottoman Empire at the end of the eighteenth century, and the Duchy of Warsaw, also known as Congress Poland. The Pale, therefore, extended from the North Sea in the north to the Black Sea in the south, a distance of some 1,200 miles and an area of nearly 500,000 square miles. By the end of the nineteenth century the Pale was home to some 45 percent of the Jews in the world.

Catherine and her officials' decision to limit where Jews could live was less motivated by the fear of Jews and their religion and more with the fact that the state had to integrate hundreds of thousands of new Jewish subjects into the empire's legal structure.[10] Officials worried that permitting Jews to move into the interior of the country could have destabilizing consequences. The settlement of Jews in regions where they had never lived might cause administrative problems as well as provoke resentment among non-Jews who would now have to compete with Jewish merchants and shopkeepers. Catherine and her advisors also worried that the presence of Jews who operated taverns, collected taxes, and managed the estates of wealthy landlords might antagonize peasants who already viewed Jews with suspicion and hostility. Officials, committed to maintaining social and political stability, also feared that peasant antagonism toward the Jews would result in violent outbursts. There was also concern that Jews might acquire control of the country's world of commerce if they could conduct business throughout the vast empire.

Although the establishment of the Pale severely constrained the geographical mobility of Jews, the ruling was not unusual in Russia; the vast majority of the tsar's subjects, particularly the enserfed peasants, also did not enjoy freedom of movement and residence. Still, the restrictions were onerous. Jews required special permission to settle in the rest of the empire, and the government even chose at various times over the course of the nineteenth century to limit where Jews could live within the Pale. On occasion the tsar decreed that Jews had to leave regions where they had lived for generations. By the end of the nineteenth century 94 percent of Jews still lived with the confines of the Pale. The remaining 6 percent, composed of certain merchants and those with university degrees, had been granted permission after 1861 to live in the empire's interior. Jewish settlement was most concentrated in the northern and western regions of the Pale, where Jews comprised 15 percent of the total population and 14 percent, respectively. The number and percentage of Jews diminished in the south and east—areas that had been opened to Jewish settlement after the Polish partitions.[11]

Jews tended to live in small market towns known as shtetls, which were scattered throughout the rural regions of the Pale of Settlement.[12] Shtetl Jews also lived in close proximity to Polish, Ukrainian, Russian, and Belarusian peasants. Jews rarely lived in isolation from non-Jews and tended to interact with Gentiles in the marketplace, stores, and streets of the shtetl. But this physical proximity did not translate into close personal and social ties, given differences in language and culture. Even though the geographic restriction limited direct contact between Jews and non-Jews throughout the country, the Jewish question nevertheless permeated society. First-hand experience with Jews was not (and is still not) a prerequisite for holding anti-Jewish prejudices and opinions.

When population growth and changes in the agrarian economy made it difficult for shtetl dwellers to make ends meet, a sizable number of them migrated to larger towns and cities such as Odesa, Vilna, and Kyiv in order to escape deteriorating conditions of shtetl life after the mid-nineteenth century. New opportunities in the professions, manufacturing, and commerce became available to Jews during the final decades of the century as the Russian economy modernized. Jews tended to be an urban people: in some towns and cities Jews made up 40, sometimes 50 percent or more of the population. For example, in Berdichev, a small city some 100 miles west of Kyiv, Jews made up 80 percent of the populace in 1897; in Odesa, the fourth-largest city in the empire in terms of population at the turn of the twentieth century, Jews comprised some 35 percent of the inhabitants. This trend to concentrate in larger urban areas intensified in the decades prior to 1914, but it did not ameliorate poverty because Jews could not relieve population pressures by moving to the interior of the Russian Empire. Nor did it alter the fact that most Jews continued to live in shtetls.[13]

Who Is a Jew?

This succinct question, which lies at the heart of the Jewish question, has no straightforward answer since the defining characteristics of being Jewish can vary depending on whether the person asking the question is a Jew or Gentile. Moreover, the answer is fluid and dynamic, changing over time and depending on the country in which the question is posed. How Russians and other non-Jews identified Jews is an important question since it shaped the thinking of Jews and non-Jews alike in both tsarist and communist Russia. It also reflected how Gentiles perceived the distinguishing features of Jews and contributed to the policies carried out by officials who tackled the issue of whether Jews could fit into non-Jewish society.

What were the markers of being a Jew? What made someone Jewish in the eyes of the state and gentile society? Did religion, language, national identity, cultural heritage, or race (notwithstanding the lack of scientific basis)—separately or in combination—determine whether someone was Jewish? Yiddish may have been the lingua franca of Jews in the Russian Empire, but Jews also knew a smattering of other languages since the Pale of Settlement was multilingual. Russians, Ukrainians, Jews, Poles, Belarussians, and Lithuanians lived in close proximity with each other and needed to find ways to communicate with each other in order to conduct business.

Two basic distinctions among the peoples of tsarist Russia were religion and language, both of which the autocratic state used to categorize its subjects. This made sense, particularly in the case of many Russian Jews, since Yiddish and Judaism, especially prior to the nineteenth century, tended to permeate all aspects of a Jew's daily life both as an individual and as a member of a community. Notions of Jewishness rooted in religion, culture, tradition, language, and sense of peoplehood—characteristics that we consider markers of ethnic and ethno-religious identity—contributed to the shaping of individual and collective Jewish identity. The rhythms of religious observance helped shape a Jew's personal, family, and communal life; one's Jewishness was, for most Jews, all-encompassing since religious strictures and laws governed one's daily life, from dress to diet, and from education to interactions with Gentiles. The Jews' worldview was circumscribed by Judaism, which was a particularly salient aspect of Jewish life.

By the late nineteenth century, however, social, economic, political, and intellectual developments had begun to rend the fabric of traditional Jewish society and prompted many Jews—both men and women—to step outside the confines of the Jewish world and participate, however haltingly, in gentile society. This was a process at work throughout Europe in the eighteenth and nineteenth centuries, when acculturation, integration, and even assimilation altered perceptions of Jewishness and broke down the barriers that tended to isolate Jews from non-Jews. During the final half-century of tsarist rule, Judaism began to play less of a role in the lives of many Russian Jews who began to view their Jewishness in ways divorced from religious observance. In other words, many Jews began to acquire an identity in which Judaism played an attenuated role. Nonetheless, the tsarist state continued to categorize Jews in terms of religion and languages.

While Jews were viewed as a religious group under the tsars, the communist state viewed them as a national minority.[14] Soviet officials jettisoned religion as the identifying feature of people living in the Soviet Union, preferring instead to categorize people by social origin and nationality, which was determined by language, culture, ethnicity, and place of residence. Given the communist regime's campaign to eradicate religion and class distinctions, it comes as no surprise that nationality served as an organizing principle in the multinational Soviet Union. One difference between tsarist and communist policies toward Jews was the active promotion of Jewish assimilation and integration into non-Jewish society. The Kremlin granted Jews full civil and political rights and, as we shall see, sometimes adopted policies designed to combat antisemitism.

Nevertheless, the Kremlin's attitude and policy toward Jews shared much in common with those of its tsarist predecessors.[15] Under tsars and communists alike, the perception of Judaism as a key element of Jewishness that undergirded Jewish behavior and needed to be purged from Jewish life remained a crucial element of the Jewish question. Moreover, the social, economic, and cultural trends affecting Russian Jews continued under communism. For example, Judaism continued to play a lesser role in the lives of Soviet Jews, particularly for young adults who fell under the sway of the Kremlin's antireligious policies. In addition, marriage between Jews and non-Jews increased as did the number of Jews who attended schools, institutes, and universities where the language of instruction was Russian and the subjects taught were wholly secular in content. Jews also began to seek employment in fields of opportunity now open to them such as the civil service. In short, Soviet Jews began to acculturate and integrate into mainstream society as their ties to traditional Jewish society weakened.

Themes

The following chapters approach the Jewish question thematically by exploring it through the prism of four sub-questions. I focus on religion, culture, the economy, and politics. My intent is not to present a full treatment of all aspects of the Jewish question. Rather, I select those key moments and details that best illustrate, to my mind, specific aspects of the Jewish question under tsars and communists. While I draw upon written texts to illustrate my argument, I also rely on visual images because they are a rich primary source for historians and illuminate the myriad ways Russians formulated the Jewish question in a society with low literacy rates. In 1897 fewer than three in ten Russians could read and write, but literacy grew to 56 percent by the mid-1920s and 75 percent by 1937 due to a concerted campaign by the communist government. It is therefore not surprising that visual images played a major role in conveying knowledge about the Jewish question. Moreover, they reveal the continuity of anti-Jewish suspicion and hatred from the eighteenth to the twentieth centuries. While the Jewish question was not static, since elements of it changed over time, its fundamental features remained consistent. The Russian Revolution of 1917 and the establishment of communist rule had less impact on the formulation of the Jewish question than we might expect, notwithstanding the momentous consequences of the collapse of the autocracy and the consolidation of power by a communist government dedicated to a radical transformation of all aspects of social, economic, political, and cultural life.

Antisemitism also merits attention since it served as the foundation of that question. In general, antisemitism is the hostility or prejudice toward Jews and Judaism, and has encompassed a wide variety of attitudes, beliefs, and behaviors since the emergence of Christianity. But by the late nineteenth century it acquired the characteristics of a political ideology and movement that targeted Jews as the purported source of myriad problems besetting European society. Antisemitic attitudes and actions in their modern variant reflected and shaped the contours of the Jewish question as it developed from the late eighteenth century onward. Antisemitism and the Jewish question were expressed in religious, cultural, socioeconomic, and political terms that reveal more about non-Jewish society than they do about Jews. While each chapter that follows is devoted to one of the categories mentioned in the previous sentence, the reader should keep in mind that the division of the Jewish question into these constituent parts is done for the sake of description and explication. In reality the various expressions of the Jewish question were not neatly delineated but leached into each other. Emphasizing one of these aspects often implicitly invoked others, making it difficult to disentangle economic grievances from political concerns. For example, economic resentments and frustrations assumed political coloration during times of revolutionary unrest and outbursts of anti-Jewish violence. The result was a conglomeration of interlocking ideas, attitudes, and policies that held Jews on both individual and community levels as a socioeconomic, national, political, and religious menace that commanded the attention of state and society, and required resolution. Moreover, studying antisemitism and the Jewish question provides insights into the nature of gentile society and tells us little about the Jews targeted by antisemites.

As the governor-general of Odesa, Count Aleksandr Dondukov-Korsakov, put it in a memorandum explaining the outbreak of anti-Jewish violence in 1881, the Jews' supposed economic stranglehold was the source of popular animus toward Jews:

> The exploitation of the local populations by the Jews, who control all sectors of trade in cities and villages ... provokes serious antipathy among the agricultural population and the lower classes of the city. The special commercial attitude that the Jews "import' to all sectors of business, even spiritual occupations, turns public opinion against them .... The Jewish question is

very severe, it is the line in the sand not only in economic but also in social and educational life.[16]

Dondukov-Korsakov also claimed that Jews, as a "cosmopolitan people with their caste-like order and exclusive tribal interests pose a serious danger not only to the economic fate of the region but also to its civil and political development." This threat necessitates "a quick, definitive, and thorough solution to the Jewish Question, which is also a general Russian question, for it touches on the most vital, material, moral, and social interests of Russia in the present and future."[17]

One historian has written that antisemitism can be understood as a "cultural code" that provided Europeans with an arsenal of ideas about the purported role Jews played in the disruptions and challenges brought about by industrialization, urbanization, democratization, and other social, cultural, and political phenomena associated with modernization since the eighteenth century.[18] The Jewish question was one way to combine the various strains of antisemitic thought and behavior into an overarching world view that attributed all the ills of modern Europe to a specific group of people regardless of place and context. Resolving the Jewish question would, in the minds of antisemites, eliminate the numerous shortcomings and difficulties of life in the modern world. "Ideas about Jews" and "pathological fantasies of Judaism" are an integral part of how non-Jews "constructed the reality of their world."[19] In other words, the Jewish question requires us to ask: What does it mean for a society to view a group of people as a fundamental threat to its well-being?[20]

One caveat is in order. This book does not claim to be a history of Jews in tsarist Russia and the Soviet Union. Nor does it discuss the historiography about Russian and Soviet Jews. My goal differs in that I set out to explore how non-Jews formulated the Jewish question. I am not concerned with how Jews defined themselves individually or collectively, or how Jewish society changed over time in late Imperial Russia and the Soviet Union. Nor do I address how Jews responded to the Jewish question except when doing so illuminates the nature of the Jewish question from the perspective of Gentiles. At times Jewish voices do make an appearance in this book, but again let me emphasize that its focus is on how non-Jews perceived the Jews living in their midst. The reader interested in the history of Jewish society and culture in all its diverse richness has to look elsewhere, and the books mentioned in footnotes and listed in the Selected Bibliography are a good place to start.

CHAPTER 1
THE RELIGIOUS QUESTION:
JUDAISM, RITUAL MURDER, AND
ATHEISM

For two millennia Christians viewed Jews with suspicion, largely because they held them responsible for the death of Christ and condemned them for not embracing him as the son of God. Moreover, they believed that Judaism, which played an important role in virtually all aspects of the daily life of traditional Jews, was morally impoverished and inspired an unrelenting, fanatical hatred for Christians and an impulse to harm, exploit, and dominate them. Christians also believed that Jews were clannish and would only attend to the interests of their co-religionists. In concert with other anti-Jewish prejudices, such predilections justified all kinds of measures to protect non-Jews from the dangers allegedly posed by Jews. Many Russians and other Gentiles shared these views, notwithstanding the fact that the overwhelming majority of them never met a Jew.

The religious question, or whether Judaism should be regarded as a baneful influence on Christian society, as articulated in tsarist Russia tended to be the foundation of many aspects of the other problems addressed in this book. It fueled anti-Jewish attitudes and behaviors in general and helped to shape and sustain the political, economic, social, and cultural questions that I discuss in later chapters. Even when religious hatred was neither openly nor obliquely voiced and even when it was masked in expressions of antisemitism that seemed removed from anti-religious animus, antagonism toward Judaism suffused the Jewish question. Yet despite the fact that negative attitudes toward Judaism actually preceded the actual presence of Jews inside the borders of the Russian Empire, the tsarist regime did not, for the most part, interfere with the religious beliefs and practices of its Jewish subjects. It is therefore appropriate to begin this book with a discussion of how and why Judaism and its teachings were at the heart of the Jewish question in Russia.

Critics of Jews and Judaism asserted that the Talmud—the compendium of rabbinic discussions and interpretations about the Hebrew Scriptures that serve as the basis of Jewish religious law, practice, and observance—was the basis of the Jews' alleged hatred of Gentiles and justified Jews' efforts to exploit non-Jews. In the late 1850s, the journalist V. R. Zotov condemned the deleterious impact of the Talmud, which, he claimed, encouraged Jews to oppress non-Jews. Several years later A. Aleksandrov penned "A Few Words about the Talmud" in which he stressed that the teachings of the Talmud fostered hatred for non-Jews, even permitting all forms of thieving and deception as well as the taking of life so long as the victim was not Jewish. According to Aleksandrov, "Judaism can be understood and perceived only in the Talmud: it now carries the whole spirit of the Jewish nation; it contains all the secrets and clues of that incomprehensible and melancholy phenomenon encompassing the life and history of this nation."[1]

Beginning in the mid-1870s, Ippolit Liutostanskii, a Catholic priest who converted to Russian Orthodoxy, began publishing diatribes that accused Jews of engaging in ritual murder, which he attributed to Judaism. In his view, all the machinations of Jews resulted from their fanatical adherence to the Talmud, which he claimed lay at the root of the Jews' impulse to dominate the world. He wrote:

> nothing more than the historical demonstration of that hatred which Jewry has nourished toward Christianity from the first moment of its appearance in the world, nothing more than the deliberate, malevolent perversion, the corruption of the Old Testament in one exclusive direction—blind, boundless hostility toward Christ and his followers.[2]

Such sentiments were not exclusively the purview of antisemitic intellectuals and journalists who argued that Jewish religious law, particularly the Talmud, sanctioned reprehensible behavior including murder. Government officials also shared the belief that Judaism lay at the root of efforts of Jews to harm non-Jews and prevented them from integrating into Russian society. In the 1840s a memorandum written under the direction of Count Pavel Kiselev, who was tasked with evaluating the legal status of Jews in the empire, blamed the "estrangement of the Jews from the general civil order" on the Talmud. According to Kiselev, Jews were intent on dominating other peoples because their status as the "Chosen People" directed them to do so.[3]

Suspicion of the Talmud was seriously misplaced since few Jews in the Russian Empire were well versed in its teachings. The religious education of Jews was limited to learning to read Hebrew and studying the Hebrew Scriptures in *kheyder*, the Jewish equivalent of a one-room elementary school. Only small numbers of Jewish men immersed themselves in the close study of the Talmud in yeshivas and rabbinical seminaries.

The belief that Jews posed an existential threat to Russians is best illustrated by the blood libel, the accusation that Jews engaged in ritual murder for religious purposes. The blood libel was a fabrication that dated back to the mid-twelfth century, when Jews in England were accused of murdering a Christian youth in order to mock the Passion of Christ. Proponents of the blood libel insisted that Judaism required Jews to engage in blood sacrifice.

The myth that Jews killed gentile youths as a religious ritual took root and spread over the subsequent centuries to the European continent, where Jews were accused of needing Christian blood, particularly that of young boys and girls, in order to perform certain religious rituals such as weddings and circumcisions. Jews also supposedly performed other practices such as Host desecration. In addition, Jews purportedly needed gentile blood to bake the unleavened bread known as matzo eaten at their annual Passover meals (seders), notwithstanding the fact that Jewish law forbids the consumption of any blood. Not surprisingly, accusations of using Christian blood for matzo tended to emerge in springtime during the Passover and Easter holidays, particularly if a young Christian boy or girl disappeared or their body was discovered.[4] Christians would accuse their Jewish neighbors of the crimes, and local authorities would imprison and even execute Jews accused of murders. The best-known blood libel prior to the twentieth century occurred in the German city of Trent in 1475, when eighteen Jewish men and women, who were subjected to brutal torture, confessed to killing a two-year-old child. They were then burned at the stake.[5]

As Jews migrated to Eastern Europe due to expulsions from German-speaking lands and the allure of economic opportunities, the blood libel came with them. Beginning in the sixteenth century, the charge of ritual murder had mostly lost currency in Western and Central Europe, but it found a receptive home in the Polish-Lithuanian Commonwealth, home to the bulk of Europe's Jews until much of it was integrated into the Russian Empire. Until the nineteenth century, tsarist Russia remained immune from the blood libel because of the absence of Jews and the lack of concern that Orthodox Christianity had for the ritual murder accusation. This did not mean, however, that the Russian Orthodox Church and its parishioners did not harbor anti-Jewish prejudices. Moreover, the incorporation of territory during the reign of Catherine the Great populated by hundreds of thousands of Jews and millions of Catholics and Uniates meant that the blood libel now became part of the social and cultural landscape of the Russian Empire.[6]

Over the course of the nineteenth century the belief that Judaism compelled Jews to engage in ritual murder had become commonplace among the populace of the Russian Empire. Rumors of blood libel abounded throughout the empire and picked up pace at the turn of the twentieth century.[7] Investigations and trials of Jews charged with murdering Christians took place in provincial villages and small towns during the 1820s, 1850s, and 1870s: the Jewish defendants were acquitted.[8] In the Russian town of Velizh in 1823, the death of a three-year-old boy whose body was mutilated and drained of blood led to accusations that Jews had killed him in order to collect his blood for religious purposes. Authorities arrested forty-three Jews for the murder and, despite the prosecution's dismissal of all charges in 1824, officials reopened the case the following year after the intercession of Tsar Nicholas I. The investigation dragged on for a decade, thereby making it the longest blood libel case in modern times, before the government dismissed all charges against the imprisoned Jews and exiled to Siberia three non-Jews for spreading the rumors about the Jews' guilt and orchestrating the campaign to bring about their arrests and prosecution.[9]

During the nineteenth century a series of books and articles appeared in Russian that explored the veracity of the accusation and made the discussion of the Jewish question inseparable from blood libel. In the 1840s an influential study affirmed the existence of ritual murder, and coverage of supposed cases of ritual murder filled the pages of many of the journals and newspapers that proliferated during the second half of the century, lending credence to the belief that Jews killed gentile children for their blood.[10]

The best- known case of blood libel occurred in the city of Kyiv on the eve of the First World War. The arrest and trial of Menachem Beilis in 1911 acquired the dubious honor of being the most publicized example of blood libel since 1475 and became a cause célèbre for Jews throughout Europe and North America.[11] Along with the trial of Captain Alfred Dreyfus in France in the 1890s and the lynching of Leo Frank in Atlanta, Georgia, in 1915, the prosecution of Beilis on trumped-up charges and manufactured evidence came to represent one of the most blatant abuses of government power in the service of antisemitism until the Third Reich. All three cases sparked spirited discussions and captivated the attention of their respective societies. They revealed deep rifts in each country's political sensibilities and cultural values and scarred the social and political landscapes, underscoring the unresolved tensions between liberal and conservative, and secular and religious values that vied for influence. The incidents also highlighted the persistence of antisemitism on both popular and official levels as high-ranking government officials in France and Russia actively participated in the railroading of two innocent men. Right-wing journalists also bore responsibility for what happened to Frank, Dreyfus, and Beilis. Finally, the Beilis affair also speaks to the impact of modernity: the trial occurred in an open courtroom with a jury deciding his fate and both prosecution and defense relied on scientific and medical evidence in the arguments.[12] While the accusation had roots in the Middle Ages, the trial was a thoroughly modern phenomenon.[13]

Beilis managed a brick factory in Kyiv, and in the summer of 1911 the police arrested him for what was believed to be the ritual slaying of Andrei Iushchinskii, a twelve-year-old boy. No evidence existed linking Beilis to the vicious murder of Iushchinskii, whose body was riddled with over four dozen knife wounds that drained most of the blood. At first the police suspected Vera Cheberiak, the leader of a gang of petty thieves. But she was a member of an antisemitic political party, and those in charge of the investigation decided to follow the urgings of vocal antisemites who claimed Iushchinskii's murder displayed the purported tell-tale signs of ritual murder. They hounded the government to turn its attention toward Jews in the hope of saving one of their own, ensuring the state's continued persecution of Jews, and promoting a virulent form of Russian nationalism.

Even though the blood libel was rooted in religious prejudices, the case against Beilis had a secular coloration that reflected concerns about the social and political stability of late Imperial Russia. Beilis's ordeal underscores how religious prejudice continued to inspire anti-Jewish attitudes and behaviors at the same time that secular concerns began to characterize the Jewish question. Like elsewhere on the European continent, by the twentieth century the Jewish question focused on the problems besetting Europe as it underwent fundamental social, economic, and political transformations. But we must remember that Judeophobia, or the fear of Jews, took sustenance from the belief that Judaism was intent on destroying Christian civilization. Hatred of Jews, particularly as manifested in the ritual murder accusation, continued to draw on theological arguments grounded not only in the deliberate misreading and misunderstanding of Judaism but also out-and-out lying and falsification.

Several police investigators, government prosecutors, and high-ranking members of the tsarist bureaucracy, including the ministers of justice and police, chose to pin the murder on Beilis for political reasons. Minister of Justice Ivan Shcheglovitov approved the plot to frame a Jew in the hope of currying favor with Tsar Nicholas II. Shcheglovitov believed that the prosecution of Beilis would provide the autocratic regime with an ideological bulwark that would bolster autocratic principles, values, and policies. This was particularly important in the aftermath of Russia's humiliating defeat at the hands of Japan in 1904–5, which undermined the autocracy's military standing and confidence. The minister joined others in reasoning that the conviction of Beilis would scuttle recent efforts to dismantle the Pale of Settlement. After all, a successful prosecution of a Jew for ritual murder would prove the evil and duplicitous nature of Jews, thereby justifying the antisemitic policies and practices of the autocracy in the face of condemnation on the world stage. At the time the regime was under intense scrutiny by foreign governments and domestic critics for their anti-Jewish policies, and the conspirators hoped that the conviction of a Jew for ritual murder would vindicate the government and prop up its image. Officials and right-wing political activists and journalists could then proclaim that ritual murder was not a fantasy but a reality acknowledged in the Russian courts, which enjoyed the respect of jurists in Europe. A guilty verdict by a jury would therefore justify the autocracy's refusal to lift legal disabilities against its Jewish subjects and abolish the Pale of Settlement, thus helping to restore the tarnished image and reputation of the tsarist regime both at home and abroad.

The conspirators settled upon Beilis as the murderer and spent over two years putting together a case against him (and other unidentified Jews) based on perjured testimony and without any forensic evidence linking the defendant to the crime. In fact, Vera Cheberiak steered the police in the direction of Beilis since she lived next to the brick factory, where her son and other neighborhood children played. The indictment focused less on connecting Beilis to the crime than on demonstrating the supposed ritual aspect of the murder. The prosecution relied on a report and testimony of Ivan Sikorskii, an eminent psychiatrist and university professor, who believed that the autopsy revealed that the killers drained Iushchinskii's body of blood in a ritualistic manner as part of a "vendetta" carried out by "the Sons of Jacob," a not very subtle reference to Jews.[14]

The trial took place in the fall of 1913, which meant that Beilis, a mild-mannered and well-liked family man, languished in jail for over two years, unable to see his wife and children and with limited contact with his lawyers. At the trial the government called as its chief witness

Father Justin Pranaitis, a disgraced Catholic priest with a shady past. Pranaitis was one of the few men of the cloth to support in public the ritual murder accusation, and his testimony at the trial revealed his nonsensical understanding of Judaism. His utterances served the purposes of the prosecution since he claimed that the Talmud sanctioned the killing of non-Jews, notwithstanding the Judaic stricture against taking a human life. Pranaitis's assertions shared much in common with the views of many Christian theologians and anti-Jewish publicists who for centuries had asserted that Judaic law encouraged not only the exploitation and oppression of Gentiles, but also their murder.

Pranaitis followed in the footsteps of other Russian antisemites who claimed that the Talmud was at the core of the Jews' behavior designed to exploit and harm Christians. According to Pranaitis's fanciful, not to mention ill-informed, reading of Jewish religious texts, the killing of Gentiles, from the perspective of Jews, would hasten the arrival of the Messiah. The priest alleged that Jews used Christian blood for magical and medicinal purposes as well as for baking matzo. Pranaitis made a fool of himself on the witness stand, and Beilis's defense team handily ripped to shreds the priest's testimony during cross-examination. Defense attorneys demonstrated his ignorance of Judaism and the Talmud, pointing out that he had difficulty reading Hebrew and that he mistranslated and misconstrued those religious texts he relied upon for his accusations.

Finally, in order to bolster its assertion that Beilis and unidentified Jews murdered Iushchinskii out of religious fanaticism, the prosecution went to ridiculous lengths to demonstrate that Beilis was a zealot engaged in a conspiracy with other religious fanatics intent on fulfilling the strictures of Judaism. Tsarist officials conveniently glossed over the fact that Beilis was not particularly observant and had attenuated ties to Judaism. After all, Beilis evidently worked on the Sabbath, the day Iushchinskii's murder took place.

As Figure 1.1 illustrates, a perverse understanding of Judaism and Jewish religious practices drove the ritual murder accusation against Beilis. The round object held by both the boy and the idol (with Beilis written above its head and wearing an ancient Egyptian headdress)

Figure 1.1 "See Yosel, this is Beilis!" in both Russian and Yiddish with Cyrillic letters

Dvuglavyi orel (The Double-Headed Eagle), no. 49 (November 24, 1913), 4. Courtesy of The Bridge Research Network

could be the Host, or sacramental bread of the Eucharist. But more likely it is a piece of matzo. In addition, the boy's gaze is directed toward the idol by someone who appears to be an elderly woman, perhaps his mother or grandmother. The knife held by the idol signifies the mortal threat purportedly posed by Jews, while the awl on the right of the drawing alludes to the weapon that investigators claimed caused the dozens of punctures found on the victim's body. The fact that several Jews are prostrate before the idol speaks to the belief that Jews worshipped the false god of Beilis.

Even though the jury acquitted Beilis of homicide, it accepted the government's assertion that Iushchinskii's death had the hallmarks of a ritual murder, thereby vindicating the autocracy's efforts to characterize Jews and Judaism as malevolent forces that deserved persecution and discriminatory treatment. It was a pyrrhic victory, however, because world opinion, especially among Jews and governments hoping the autocracy would implement liberal reforms, viewed the trial as a travesty of justice. Rather than convince foreign governments that the autocracy's treatment of Jews was justified, the prosecution of Beilis on trumped-up charges embarrassed the regime and confirmed the view that Tsar Nicholas II's government was a bastion of antisemitism with nothing but contempt for the rule of law. The trial led to more, not less, scrutiny of the state's discriminatory treatment of Jews.

To be sure, many non-Jews welcomed the acquittal of Beilis, who found supporters in unusual quarters. Beilis wrote in his memoir *The Story of My Sufferings* that the captain of the police station who processed his release welcomed him warmly, notwithstanding the fact that the captain was, in the words of Beilis, "a notorious ... anti-Semite ... and could not endure the sight of a Jew." The captain asked Beilis if he would meet with the captain's daughter who wanted to congratulate him on his release from prison. The daughter, according to her father, "wept like a child" and "neglected her studies" because of the ordeal Beilis endured. When Beilis met the daughter, she told him she and her friends "suffered so much because of you .... We did not sleep whole nights; and always talked of your sufferings, but of course it was nothing compared to what you have gone through. But now, justice and truth have won out. I wish you peace and happiness together with your family."[15]

The blood libel accusation subsided but did not vanish after the collapse of the autocracy. In the 1920s and 1930s a handful of accusations of ritual murder occurred in different regions of the Soviet Union and resulted in physical attacks on Jews. Officials and police on the local level sometimes supported efforts to blame Jews for the disappearance of a boy or girl. But the communist government, committed—for the most part—to weeding out antisemitism and combating open expressions of the ritual murder accusation, stepped in to ensure that trials did not take place and Jews were not punished. Still, the belief was especially durable, and the Soviet government was unable to stamp it out. Indeed, it may have contributed to antisemitism's persistence because official attacks on Judaism frequently emphasized two rituals: circumcision and kosher butchering, both of which involved knives and bloodletting. Banning such practices and trying to discredit them through propaganda ironically kept alive popular associations of Jews with the blood libel.[16]

In the Soviet period, from the perspective of the Kremlin, Judaism, like all religions, endangered the building of socialism. Communism was a secular ideology determined to stamp out organized religious belief and practice because, in the words of Karl Marx and Friedrich Engels, "religion is the opiate of the people" that enabled the political and economic exploitation and domination of workers by capitalists and the governments that did their bidding. Soviet officials believed that organized religion, a sign of cultural backwardness, prevented the acceptance of communist values and hindered the desire and ability of citizens to take advantage of the economic and educational opportunities that opened up during the first two decades after the collapse of tsardom.

In the Soviet Union the fledgling communist regime did not single out Judaism for special treatment. The campaign against religion affected all faiths in the Soviet Union. In the 1920s and 1930s Soviet authorities engaged in an aggressive offensive to close churches, synagogues, and mosques, sometimes turning them into warehouses, workers' clubs, and even interrogation centers for the secret police. Places of worship tended to be the only places where religious Jews, Muslims, and Russian Orthodox believers could assemble outside the confines of the family and private homes. The Kremlin also persecuted clerics and shut down seminaries in an effort to interfere with religious observance and the ability to pass on religious knowledge and practice to a new generation.

The regime outlawed all forms of official and legal discrimination against Jews. But simultaneously, and in contradictory fashion, in the twenty or so years after the 1917 revolution, the communist regime closed synagogues, forbade the publication of prayer books and other religious texts, outlawed the teaching of and publishing in Hebrew, shut the doors of yeshivas where Jewish men immersed themselves in the study of the Torah and Talmud and prepared themselves for the rabbinate, and harassed, hounded, and often arrested rabbis. Authorities also suppressed the activities of persons who played indispensable roles in religious life: kosher butchers, cantors, and mohels who performed circumcisions. In addition, the authorities made it difficult for Jews to observe the Sabbath and other religious holidays.

For the most part the anti-Judaism campaign was carried out by Jewish communists who conducted their agitation and propaganda efforts in Yiddish, a sign that many Soviet Jews were more proficient in Yiddish than Russian. Moreover, the Communist Party evidently felt that Jews were more likely to respond to other Jews seeking to undermine religious life. These activists organized meetings and lectures in factories and even staged theatrical performances in which Judaism, rabbis, Jewish customs and practices, and teachers of Hebrew were put on "mock trial." The judges invariably found the "defendants" guilty and sentenced them to death. Other public activities included the organization of dances and other forms of entertainment on religious holidays such as Yom Kippur and Rosh Hashanah as a way to lure Jewish youths away from organized religion by emphasizing how Judaism promoted capitalism and the exploitation of the poor. As one antireligious publication noted, observant Jews believed that "capitalism rules over body and soul" and built altars from "gold and silver."[17]

Another propaganda practice involved conducting alternative Passover seders with so-called Red Haggadahs that told the story of the Jews' exodus from Egypt in terms of class conflict and the victory of communism. The goal was not only to undermine traditional religious observance, but also to promote communist ideology. Seder rituals and prayers were transformed into attacks on capitalism. For example, the prayer said when washing one's hands was rewritten as follows: "Wash off all the bourgeois mud, wash off the mold of generations, and do not say a blessing but a curse. Devastation must come upon all the old rabbinical laws and customs."[18] The traditional Haggadah's emphasis on the Jews' liberation from the oppression of the Pharoah was replaced, in the Red Haggadah, with "deliverance from the slavery of capitalism." The Passover story as narrated by the Kremlin proclaimed: "May all the aristocrats, bourgeois, and their helpers ... and other counter-revolutionaries—be consumed in the fire of revolution."[19] In the Soviet version, Jews were "slaves of capitalism until October came and led us out of the land of exploitation with a strong hand, and if it were not for October, we and our children would still be slaves." Rather than ending the seder with the hope that world Jewry will gather "next year in Jerusalem," Red Haggadahs proclaimed that "world revolution" would characterize the upcoming year.[20]

In the 1920s and 1930s the Kremlin also tried to weaken religious observance among the Soviet Union's some two and a half million Jews through "softer" measures such as the printed word and visual imagery.[21] The government spearheaded the campaign against Judaism by publishing antireligious posters and books, pamphlets, and journals. Antireligious activists relied on the power of the word and image to express their message that Judaism served the interests of the Jewish bourgeoisie intent on exploiting the vast majority of Soviet Jews who eked out meager livelihoods. In the 1920s Soviet propaganda tried to foment class conflict within Jewish society by depicting religious Jews as obstacles to the building of socialism and the march of history. Rabbis were shown as willing accomplices of the Jewish bourgeoisie whose machinations were intended to exploit Jewish workers in order to buttress the socioeconomic standing of the well-to-do. Certain articles of clothing such as shoes with spats, hats, and tuxedos served as markers for class and religiosity. Even body type was significant, with capitalist Jews depicted as overfed and self-satisfied. Jewish proletarians were invariably depicted as male (as were Jewish entrepreneurs), though significant numbers of Jewish women worked in handicraft workshops and even small factories. Generally portrayed as weak and defenseless, male Jewish workers developed muscles and heroic qualities if they possessed the political consciousness needed to join the ranks of the socialist revolution.

According to antireligious artists and writers, rabbis did more than just the bidding of the capitalist exploiters of the common Jew: the complex set of Jewish dietary laws and rituals worked to keep the average Jew impoverished, while ensuring that rabbis and others lived well. For example, religious dictates for the Passover holiday required Jews to clean their kitchens of all food that was not deemed kosher for the holiday. The added expense of buying new food was compounded by the fact that rabbis frequently enjoyed a monopoly on the sale of Passover items, particularly the special flour for baking matzo. As the antireligious activists saw it, these unnecessary extra expenses went directly into the rabbis' pockets. This system of religious directives, they argued, served only to keep the rank-and-file Jew downtrodden and beholden to religious authorities, thereby contributing to the socioeconomic and political oppression of capitalism. The aura of doing God's work and the authority of the rabbis, they asserted, supported a system in which workers obeyed employers unquestioningly and accepted poor living and working conditions.

Figure 1.2 shows a rabbi whose religious ministrations were helping a rich Jew steal from a worker who is holding the Torah and is unaware of his victimization. The text, which is a play on the verb *to purify* or *to cleanse*, has a rabbi telling the victim to "purify" his heart" while the bourgeois proclaims "So I can clean out your pockets."[22]

In a similar fashion Figure 1.3 shows, from left to right, Allah, the Christian god assisted by Jesus, Jehovah, and Buddha attending

Figure 1.2 "Purify your heart"

Bezbozhnik u stanka (The Atheist at the Work Bench), no. 8 (1925), 8. Courtesy of The Bridge Research Network

Figure 1.3 "Religion is, always and everywhere, a weapon of class rule"

Bezbozhnik u stanka (The Atheist at the Work Bench), no. 5 (1924), 10. Courtesy of The Bridge Research Network

to their respective flocks.[23] Behind each deity stands a capitalist literally holding the tethers attached to each god's congregants. The message is clear: the capitalists control society and use religion to instill obedience among believers. The caption reads: "Religion is, always and everywhere, a weapon of class rule. Religion helps the ruling classes control the thoughts of workers for whatever benefits the ruling classes."

Yet another illustration (Figure 1.4) depicts the Jewish middle class and clergy as avaricious, hypocritical, and self-serving. In the left panel the one-eyed, thick-lipped Jehovah with his hands held in the Priestly Benediction watches over Yom Kippur services.[24] In the right panel Jehovah is unmasked as a double-chinned Jewish capitalist, complete with spats and ample girth, who is gorging himself on roast pig and wine on Yom Kippur, a violation of religious proscriptions. The hands, which are represented as gloves carved (or molded) in the shape of the Priestly Benediction, hang on a coat rack, while a mask representing Jehovah lies casually on the floor.

Peering through the window are two workers who seem amused by their discovery of the capitalist's deception. In this drawing the Jewish capitalist has disguised himself as the Jewish god, thereby illustrating how Judaism is an elaborate sham that ensures the servility of the community. Judaism fosters acceptance of the status quo and secures

Figure 1.4 *Yom Kippur*

Bezbozhnik u stanka (The Atheist at the Work Bench), no. 6 (1923). Courtesy of The Bridge Research Network

the ability of the well-to-do Jewish bourgeoisie not only to live well but also to flout hypocritically religious norms. The bourgeoisie's artifice reflects the communist belief that observant Jews pray to an illusionary god, a god who has no independent existence outside the self-serving machinations of the bourgeoisie. The fact that the capitalist, a class enemy of the revolution, wears a mask to deceive those whom he exploits points to the Bolsheviks' preoccupation with political transparency. The fear that socialism's enemies concealed their true selves dominated the Kremlin's thinking and characterized the political witch hunts of the 1920s and 1930s. The regime exhorted society to unmask the enemies of the people in order to expose these efforts to fool workers.

In Figure 1.5, entitled *Children of One God*, a Jewish shoe store owner wearing a prayer shawl and phylacteries[25] exhorts his dejected worker with the following declaration: "You are a Jew, and I am a

Figure 1.5 *Children of One God*

Bezbozhnik u stanka (The Atheist at the Work Bench), no. 11 (1925), 9. Courtesy of The Bridge Research Network

Jew: we are the children of one God. You toil, and I will trade. This is the way it should be. Jehovah wants it this way. But if you sell to the atheist goyim and listen to them, then misfortune will befall us, the Jews, and Jehovah." The reference to selling to "the atheist goyim" is a not-too-subtle jibe at the supposed clannishness of Jews. Watching

Figure 1.6 *Jehovah* (spelled backward)

Bezbozhnik u stanka (The Atheist at the Work Bench), no. 8 (1923), 12. Courtesy of The Bridge Research Network

over the Jewish shopkeeper is a one-eyed Jewish god with two fangs, a reminder of the supposed blood-sucking tendencies of Jewish businessmen (the significance of the single eye is discussed below). The worker's gnarled, calloused hands stand in sharp contrast to the smooth hands of his boss.

In a similar vein, Figure 1.6 depicts a religious Jewish industrialist, decked out in all the signs of a typical Jewish fat cat (prayer shawl, phylacteries, sidelocks, spats, top hat, distended stomach, and watch fob) praying to Jehovah (spelled in reverse), who appears as a heavenly visage emanating from the smokestacks of the factories in the background. Once again Jehovah has only one eye and possesses the other attributes of the Jewish god rendered by artists, namely sidelocks, beard, prayer shawl, phylacteries, and the sign of the Priestly Benediction.

The caption is drawn from the passages in Deuteronomy and Leviticus that refer to Jehovah's selection of the Jews as the chosen people and God's promise to protect them. The illustration suggests that the Jewish bourgeoisie has agreed to worship Jehovah in exchange for protection and status. Not surprisingly, this agreement allows the industrialist to vanquish the Jewish worker, who is barefoot and unable to stand up to the wealthy businessman. Curiously, the capitalist is kneeling in prayer before Jehovah as a way to subdue the worker. The kneeling may allude to the injunction against Jews kneeling before false gods.

What are we to make of the Jewish god with a single eye? Such a depiction conjures up several allusions, and so it is difficult to know with certainty what the artists had in mind and how readers viewed the images. The single eye could refer to the all-seeing and all-knowing Jehovah. The Jewish god has no physical manifestation, but the single eye may represent the unity that Jehovah embodies. Or it might be an allusion to the belief that Jehovah is watching over the Jews, an image probably gleaned from the passage in the Midrash (commentary on texts from the Hebrew Scriptures) where it is stated that the Jewish god has one eye for this purpose. For example, in some German synagogues one eye above the Ark where the Torah is kept means that God is watching over the Jews. A single eye also appears on tombstones in Jewish cemeteries. On the other hand, the single eye may be nothing other than an expression of the evil eye. Russian popular culture is rich in the imagery of the evil eye, which can symbolize envy, jealousy, hatred, and even stinginess.[26] They may have simply been giving into the (not-wholly-unfounded) sentiment that religious Jews wished the worst for the Bolsheviks. But the fact that the *New Shorter Oxford English Dictionary* notes that "single-eyed" connotes sincerity, straightforwardness, and honesty only serves to highlight that the single eye has contradictory meanings and casts doubt on the conviction that the one-eyed Jehovah possesses the evil eye.[27] Just as we cannot know what the artists responsible for these drawings had in mind, the artists also could not be sure that readers would share their understanding of the single eye.

Orthodox Russians were accustomed to seeing images of a single eye as late as the nineteenth century. Russian icon painters painted the *velikii glaz* (the great eye) on icons and wrote the word "God" underneath as a way to capture the viewer's attention.[28] The artists could, therefore, draw freely upon the vast repository of visual imagery in Russian religious and political culture, though there is no way to ascertain whether their audience grasped the messages intended by the artists. It is likely that gentile artists drew upon this repository of folk belief rather than the more arcane and unfamiliar territory of Judaism. Moreover, Russia's religious culture and legacy continued to have resonance after 1917.

One other interpretation of the single eye also suggests itself, namely that of the association between Freemasonry and Judaism. Freemasonry traces its origins to fraternal, mutual-aid societies formed in the Middle Ages, and Freemasons are bound by oath to live lives dedicated to truth, charity, and morality. Given their secrecy and use of symbols, Freemasons came under attack by the Vatican and various European governments who suspected them of subversive activities. Since some Freemason organizations welcomed Jews as members, detractors of Freemasonry alleged that Jews had seized control of the movement in their effort to dominate Christian society.[29] A familiar symbol of the Freemasons was the single eye, also known as the Eye of Providence, best known to Americans as the one in the pyramid on the back of the dollar bill.[30] During the nineteenth and in the early twentieth century, conservative political forces and antisemites alike fostered the fiction that a worldwide Judeo-Masonic conspiracy existed. Such a belief circulated throughout Europe, and no doubt found a receptive home among some of Russia's educated public. After 1917 enemies of the communist regime condemned the supposed Judeo-Masonic conspiracy as the cause of the revolutionary upheaval that engulfed the country in 1917. Nevertheless, the Bolsheviks found it politically useful to label Freemasons as enemies of the revolution. Artists may have drawn upon this popular association of Jews and Freemasons in their effort to denigrate both Judaism and Freemasonry as counterrevolutionary forces.

The association of Jews with big noses is a timeworn, antisemitic stereotype, and the appearance of this image is not surprising in Figure 1.7. It is also worth noting that Allah also has a larger-than-life nose, thereby suggesting that Jews and Muslim Arabs shared a Semitic physiognomy in the eyes of the artists drawing for the journal. But what is the meaning of depicting the nose as a closed fist with the thumb extending between the second and third fingers? This imagery refers to the *mano in fico* (the "fig" hand) that we encountered in the introduction and alludes to how both tsarist and Soviet publications from opposing sides of the political spectrum drew upon a common reservoir of visual depictions of Jews and sentiments about the Jewish question. Portraying the Jewish god with an outlandish nose imbues the drawing with a nonhuman monstrous quality.

Figure 1.8 (The Shaven God) appeared in 1927 and depicts a single-eyed Jehovah who is linked to a not-so-subtle criticism of the New Economic Policy (known as NEP), which permitted small-scale market capitalism for most of the 1920s. Many Bolsheviks criticized NEP for strengthening capitalism and hindering the building of socialism by promoting market relations and private enterprise and trade. In particular, they characterized "Nepmen" as taking advantage of imbalances in supply and demand, and making exorbitant profits by providing urban inhabitants with food and other commodities. Given the popular association of the Jew as a capitalist who was willing to overcharge customers, it is not surprising that Jehovah (in this instance Jehovah is not spelled in reverse as it is in other drawings) sports a cravat bearing the inscription "Nepman." Again, the chronological divide between tsarist and communist eras meant little when it came to perceiving Jews as capitalists who exploit others. As one historian of NEP writes, "the stereotypical, odious private trader was often assumed to be Jewish, and thus antisemitism and popular aversion to the Nepmen fed on each other."[31]

What makes Figure 1.8 stand out is its stress on the connection between Judaism and capitalist exploitation. While Jews were condemned as Nepmen elsewhere in the press and public discussions, this explicit link between religion and the perceived shortcomings

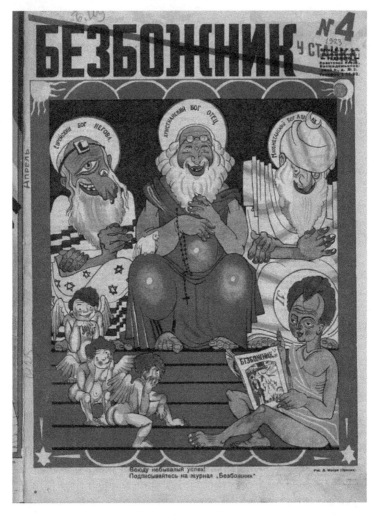

Figure 1.7 "Unparalleled success everywhere! subscribe to the journal *Bezbozhnik*"

Bezbozhnik u stanka (The Atheist at the Work Bench), no. 4 (1923), cover. Courtesy of The Bridge Research Network

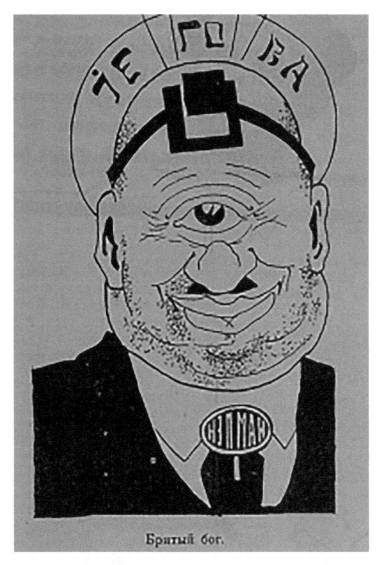

Figure 1.8 The Shaven God

Bezbozhnik u stanka (The Atheist at the Work Bench), no. 11 (1927), 19. Courtesy of The Bridge Research Network

of NEP is rooted in more than the belief that Jews were inordinately involved in commerce. The appearance of this drawing owes much to a dispute raging within the party regarding the future of NEP and is clearly designed to stimulate hostility to NEP by highlighting the Jewish connection.

Religious Jews and their god frequently assumed freakish, devil-like, and nonhuman physical characteristics in drawings and caricatures. These depictions of congregants did more than poke fun and have a laugh at the expense of organized religion. They were vicious and unforgiving in their attack on the adherents of Judaism, marking Jews as alien and monstrous. The association of Jews with monsters dates back to medieval Europe and emphasizes Christianity's "religious polemic" with not only Judaism but also Islam.[32] Such visual representations were an effective way of dehumanizing as well as demonizing religious Jews and stressing how Judaism purportedly stood in the way of building socialism.

The invasion of the Soviet Union by Germany in June 1941, however, led to a relaxation of the Kremlin's attack on Judaism and other religions. Realizing that it had to rely on religious institutions to rally the Soviet populace behind the war effort, the regime loosened its grip on the ability of churches, mosques, and synagogues to minister to the needs of their congregants, many of whom had turned to religion for comfort and spiritual guidance. During the war, which saw the death of some twenty-six million Soviet citizens, including two million Jews living in the Soviet Union, the government backed away from its suppression of Judaism. The Kremlin allowed Jews to reestablish official congregations that had been banned and also returned some synagogues that had been requisitioned by the state. A hands-off approach continued to characterize the state's treatment of organized Jewish religious life for several years after the end of the Second World War: the doors of many synagogues that had opened during the war remained opened. Officials also tolerated commemoration of the deaths of tens of thousands of Jews at Babyn Yar in Kyiv for several years after the end of hostilities, and even permitted the establishment of a rabbinical seminary in the 1950s, the first such institution authorized since the communist takeover in 1917.[33]

Despite these policies, most Soviet Jews avoided organized Jewish life out of fear of arrest and persecution, particularly beginning in 1948 when the government began to orchestrate an openly antisemitic campaign against prominent Jewish cultural figures, and the Kremlin also repressed various expressions of Jewish life and culture such as the shuttering of schools where Yiddish was a language of instruction, closing Yiddish theaters, and prohibiting discussion of the Holocaust. As we shall see in Chapter 4, the Kremlin executed over a dozen Jewish writers, poets, journalists, and academics in 1952. And yet the Kremlin did not entirely reverse its relatively lax policies toward the practice of Judaism, notwithstanding the ominous political atmosphere that characterized the final years of Stalin's life, who died in 1953.

What accounts for the paradoxical reluctance of the Soviet government after the Second World War to attack the Jewish religion while it was engaging in public attacks on other aspects of Jewish life and culture? Since the Kremlin continued its relative lax policies toward organized religious life in general (with the exception of Catholicism) after the war, it chose to refrain from attacking Judaism in order to maintain a consistent religious policy and avoid criticism from other governments. The fact that organized Jewish religious life in terms of functioning synagogues and the number of rabbis and worshippers was not significant prompted government officials to conclude that it was not worth their effort to attack Judaism. More importantly, the Kremlin wanted to use rabbis to propagate government policies and reasoned that religious observance in the niggardly number of synagogues in operation, which were subject to state supervision and observation, was "preferable to worship in private homes."[34]

It was not until the late 1950s and early 1960s that the Soviet government, at the behest of Nikita Khrushchev (ruled 1956–64), who succeeded Stalin after a brief jockeying for power among the party elite, redoubled efforts to weaken all organized religion. It closed many churches and synagogues that had opened during the war and launched a major propaganda campaign, which included active police harassment to deter younger Soviet citizens from attending religious services. The attacks on Judaism focused on how it promoted Jewish nationalism in the form of active support of Israel, with dozens of books and pamphlets appearing that stressed the political unreliability of Soviet Jews. The regime also cracked down on the baking of matzo and closely monitored the comings and goings of people who risked attending synagogue services. Unlike the 1920s and 1930s when Jewish communists carried out the attacks on Judaism in Yiddish, the audience of the anti-Jewish propaganda and agitation of the Khrushchev period was not Soviet Jewry. Rather, the Kremlin made the conscious decision to focus the anti-Jewish campaign on non-Jews by publishing books, pamphlets, and newspaper articles in languages such as Russian and Ukrainian that the general Soviet reading public could understand.[35] This attack on Judaism occurred in the aftermath of the Soviet Union's change in its policy toward Israel. The Kremlin was a strong advocate of the establishment of the State of Israel and was the first state to recognize the Jewish state's independence. By the 1950s, however, it shifted gears and took a pro-Arab, anti-Israel, and anti-Zionist stance.

One book in particular, *Judaism without Embellishment*, was especially virulent in its slanderous anti-Jewish rhetoric and drawings reminiscent of Nazi propaganda. Published in 1963 by Trofim Kichko, the book stated in no uncertain terms that Judaism was intimately linked to Zionism and served the interests of the Jewish bourgeoisie. Kichko's attack on Judaism not only borrowed freely from *The Protocols of the Elders of Zion*, a fabricated book published in 1903 that claimed Jews were engaged in a conspiracy to dominate Christian society.[36] In Kichko's words, "Jehovah delivered all of the wealth of non-Jews to the use of the Jews" and commanded Jews to exploit non-Jews. He added that "the Talmud morally corrupts people, instilling in them the spirit of commerce and extortion." According to Kichko, Judaism "is the translation of trade and commerce into religious language."[37] Moreover, Kichko linked Jewish capitalists to American imperialism, likening Zionism and Israeli policy toward Arabs to Nazi racism. The following drawing (Figure 1.9), which appeared in Kichko's book, shows David Ben-Gurion, Israel's first prime minister, erasing the word "not" from the Ten Commandments, thereby turning strictures against unethical behavior into endorsements of such behavior. Thus, "thou shalt not kill" becomes "thou shalt kill."

Figure 1.9 The Ten Commandments

See Moshe Decter, "Judaism without Embellishment': Recent Documentation of Russian Anti-Semitism." Reprinted from New Politics: A Quarterly Journal of Socialist Thought (1963), 108. Courtesy of *New Politics: A Quarterly Journal of Socialist Thought*

****

Tsarist and communist officials were concerned that Judaism, like all religions, posed a threat to the population's well-being. In the case of the autocracy, the government worried that it would undermine the values undergirding Christian society; in the case of Soviet Union, the regime fixated on the class threat posed by rabbis and the Jewish bourgeoisie. In an ideal world, reasoned tsarist and communist policymakers, Judaism would disappear as a factor in the lives of Jews. But unlike the autocracy, the communist government adopted active and aggressive measures to destroy the role played by religion in the lives of Soviet Jews by marshalling the repressive forces of the state to create a secular society devoted to the building of socialism. In such a world there would be no place for any organized religion or religious values.

Nevertheless, many Soviet Jews managed to keep alive knowledge of Jewish history, culture, and religion. They circumcised their sons, taught their children about Jewish history, and held secret bar mitzvahs. Moreover, ethnic identification as Jews remained high. But by the time the Soviet Union dissolved in 1991, most Soviet Jews knew next to nothing about Judaism and Jewish culture. The Kremlin's hope had become a reality as Soviet Jewry's ties to Judaism had become attenuated, if not non-existent. For most Jews living in the Soviet Union at the end of the twentieth century, their religious observance had become nothing more than eating matzo distributed by synagogues.

Several factors accounted for this development. One was the impact of the Holocaust, which wiped out entire communities of religious Jews, weakened the hold of Judaism on those Soviet Jews fortunate to survive the genocide, and spelled the death knell of religious life among Soviet Jewry. The physical destruction of synagogues and other institutional structures needed for religious life, coupled with the deaths of rabbis, cantors, and teachers, made it difficult for Judaism to survive after the war. The second factor was the Kremlin's unwillingness to countenance any expression of religious belief and practice, notwithstanding the easing of repressive government policies during and after the war. As we have seen, the antireligious policies of the communist regime in the 1920s and 1930s had already dramatically curtailed the ability of Judaism to function. Coupled with the impact of the war and Khrushchev's antireligious campaign of the late 1950s and early 1960s, the state's efforts succeeded in eliminating organized religion from the daily lives of all Soviet citizens. Finally, Jews living under communism became assimilated and integrated into the wholly secular society that communism set out to create. Thus, the combined impact of government policies, world war, and social and cultural transformation removed religion from the lives of Soviet Jews. But this development did not mean that the religious question disappeared. The Jews' religious heritage was still seen by the government and many in society as a threat to the stability, integrity, and health of society.

CHAPTER 2
THE CULTURAL QUESTION: ACCOMMODATION, ACCULTURATION, AND INTEGRATION

One crucial aspect of the "Jewish question" centered on the charge that Jews comprised an insular community that did not want to fit into mainstream society. Critics of Russian and Soviet Jewry pointed to the distinctive elements of Jewish society that kept Jews separate from non-Jews: not only did religious beliefs and practices mark Jews as different, but the clothes many wore and Yiddish, the language they spoke, and the food they ate underscored the extent to which they were unwilling to integrate into gentile society. Jewish education emphasized the study of Judaism to the exclusion of secular, non-religious subjects, while dietary restrictions and a host of other strictures limited social interaction between Jews and their non-Jewish neighbors, thereby creating a seemingly unbridgeable chasm between the two groups. The persistence of traditional values and culture among most Russian Jews reinforced the belief that they could not and did not want to become part of gentile society.

Nevertheless, many Jews and non-Jews rubbed shoulders on a daily basis as they conducted business and plied their trades in the neighborhoods of shtetls, towns, and cities. In particular, Jewish women interacted with Gentiles in the shops and stalls of marketplaces, while Jewish men had contact with non-Jews as they traveled the countryside as itinerant traders or served as middleman between the countryside and town. Yiddish may have been the lingua franca of Jews in tsarist Russia, but Jews also knew a smattering of other languages since the Pale of Settlement was multilingual. Russians, Ukrainians, Belarussians, Jews, Poles, and Lithuanians lived in proximity with each other and needed to find ways to communicate with each other in order to conduct business.

The incorporation of hundreds of thousands of Jews as subjects of the Russian crown in the late eighteenth century prompted the tsarist government to take stock of this new—and unwanted—minority and develop policies toward it. The creation of the Pale of Settlement was one consequence of this concern. But alongside this effort to limit contact between Jews and their neighbors, policymakers also developed measures to bring about *sblizhenie*, or the coming together of Jews and Russians through the Russification and integration of Jewry into mainstream society.

The effort to bridge the gap between Russians and Jews can be traced to the process of emancipation as it took shape across Western and Central Europe in the eighteenth and nineteenth centuries. Beginning in the mid-eighteenth century many government officials and intellectuals throughout Europe argued that Jews had to undertake reforms in their way of life in order to be accepted by non-Jewish society. In 1782 Emperor Joseph II, ruler of the Habsburg lands, issued an "Edict of Tolerance" that lifted restrictions on Jews in order to encourage their integration. The hope was to smooth the way for greater involvement of Jews in the economy, culture, and society of the empire. The stated goal was "to make the Jewish nation useful and serviceable to the State, mainly through better education and enlightenment of its youth as well as by directing them to the sciences, the arts and the crafts."[1] But along with permission for Jews to pursue livelihoods in commercial and handicraft ventures from which they were excluded, the decree enacted restrictions on the use of Yiddish and Hebrew in official documents and published materials.

This quid pro quo found expression elsewhere in Europe. The extension of rights of citizenship to Jews tended to be predicated on the willingness of Jews to demonstrate that they merited legal equality, civil rights, and political freedom. That is, Jews had to show that they wanted to integrate and acculturate into European society by learning the languages of the host societies, educating their children in secular subjects, jettisoning attitudes and behaviors that separated Jews and Gentiles, and pursuing occupations such as farming and handicraft production. In France Jewish men, who had been granted the right to vote and acquired full civil and legal equality in the aftermath of the French Revolution, were expected to speak French and become like all other French men and women in terms of dress, occupation, education, and culture. Leaders of the French Jewish community advocated that Jews should demonstrate their gratitude to the French state. In 1791 Berr Isaac Berr, a wealthy Jewish merchant and banker, wrote that "French ought to be the Jews' mother tongue." He also urged French Jews to earn "honourable" livings by becoming productive workers as manual laborers and artisans. French Jews should repay the trust shown by the revolutionary government by jettisoning those aspects of Jewish life that distinguished Jews from Gentiles.[2]

While conversion to Christianity was not a requirement to acquire the right to vote in France and elsewhere in Europe, Jews had to demonstrate that their political allegiances were, first and foremost, to the societies and states in which they lived. Their religious preference was a matter of personal choice and did not factor into whether they deserved rights of citizenship. They had to commit to becoming citizens whose primary loyalty was not to other Jews and the restoration of a politically sovereign Jewish state in the Land of Israel. In other words, Jewishness was reduced to religious affiliation, to the practice of Judaism that would not interfere with one's standing as a citizen.

Some Jewish intellectuals and community leaders also advocated acculturation and integration into gentile society, particularly in German-speaking Central Europe. Known as the *Haskalah* (Jewish enlightenment), this movement aimed at ending the isolation of Jews from gentile society by transforming their social, cultural, and economic make-up. Learning secular subjects such as math, science, literature, history, and languages would facilitate the Jews' efforts to fit in and strengthen the case for the extension of freedom and equality. One well-known proponent of Haskalah was Moses Mendelssohn, a German rabbi who, in the 1770s and 1780s, translated the Hebrew scriptures into German and encouraged Jews to pursue a secular education without sacrificing their ties to Judaism. His hope was to promote the acceptance of Jews, who he believed could contribute to cultural and intellectual life.[3]

During the nineteenth century successive tsars in Russia followed in the footsteps of other European governments to promote the cultural transformation of Jews, but they offered crucial variations on these Western and Eastern European themes. As in the rest of Europe, the hope was to bring about the acculturation of Jews. But unlike most of their counterparts in Western and Central Europe, tsarist authorities adopted both voluntary and coercive measures. Nor did officials offer Jews the "reward" of full legal and civil equality since Russia remained staunchly autocratic, with political sovereignty residing in the person of the tsar. Tsarist policy toward Jews was contradictory: it combined efforts to integrate selectively Jews into non-Jewish society with attempts to keep them separate by promulgating legislation that hindered the ability of Jews to integrate.[4] Policies could work at cross-purposes and make the application of legislation confusing and ineffectual. The see-saw nature of tsarist policy, which characterized treatment of Jews until the collapse of the Romanov dynasty in 1917, pointed to the regime's difficulty in deciding which approach to embrace. It reflected the complex nature of the Jewish question since authorities wanted to safeguard the non-Jewish subjects of the empire from the perceived exploitative proclivities of Jews, while at the same time adopting policies designed to break down the cultural, social, and economic differences between Jews and non-Jews.

One of the most aggressive and coercive measures intended to integrate Jews occurred under the regime of Tsar Nicholas I (ruled 1825–55), who implemented a draconian policy that involved conscripting Jewish boys as young as twelve into military colonies in order to wean them from Judaism.[5] He hoped that their removal from the Jewish community would transform the Jewish conscripts into loyal subjects and lead to conversion and the eventual disappearance of Judaism from the empire. The fact that military service lasted twenty-five years afforded the military ample time to undermine the Jewish youths' observance of Judaism. Estimates place the number of Jews conscripted during the reign of Nicholas II at approximately 70,000, of which 50,000 were under the age of eighteen. Military officers tended to ignore the government's assurance that Jewish recruits would be allowed to practice their faith and pursued aggressive policies to convert those under their command. One Jewish convert claimed that he embraced Orthodoxy after his commanding officers beat him and forced him "to walk barefoot on hot coals."[6] Thousands of Jewish teenagers in the military did convert, largely as a result of coercion, as did a significant number of Jewish men. The forced conversions of Jewish youths ended after Nicholas I's death in 1855, and Jews were, for the most part, free to practice Judaism as they saw fit.

But some conscripts refused to turn their backs on their religious heritage and upbringing and chose to resist by committing suicide, sometimes in groups. Still others maimed themselves by chopping off fingers and toes in order to avoid service. Not surprisingly, well-to-do Jewish families managed to keep their sons from conscription by bribing communal leaders responsible for providing the military with lists of eligible Jewish youths. Fear of conscription gave rise to the phenomenon of wealthy families hiring kidnappers (*khappers* in Yiddish) to seize Jewish adolescents from families in other communities to serve in place of their children. *Khappers* plied their trade with impunity as they abducted young Jew boys walking in public. They were known to enter into houses where they would grab boys, gag them, and drag them outside for delivery to the Jews who had hired the kidnappers. Even ordinary Jews would seize Jewish youngsters and hand them over to *khappers* as substitutes for relatives on the list of Jews destined for conscription. In one incident a woman with two small children went begging for bread. She went into a store where the shop owner had his son grab one of the children, who was then sold to *khappers*.[7]

Nicholas I's goal was "integration through enlightenment," notwithstanding his desire "to see the Jews embrace the Orthodox Christian faith en masse."[8] The tsar tempered his policy of coerced conversion with "softer" approaches, deploying the proverbial carrot to counter the deeply resented stick. At the same time that he antagonized and alienated his Jewish subjects with the draft and pressure to convert their sons, Nicholas I also took some steps to reduce the cultural distance between Jews and Gentiles by promoting the former's integration into non-Jewish society through the adoption of knowledge, skills, and occupations needed to fit in.

Beginning in the 1840s Nicholas I turned toward educational reform: he had his officials set up a system of state-financed schools for Jewish boys that, he hoped, would weaken the hold of religious education on the Jewish community.[9] The publicly financed schools taught secular subjects (Russian language, geography, history, arithmetic, and natural science) along with courses on Jewish law, history, and Hebrew Scriptures. The secular curriculum was designed to pull Jews away from traditional Jewish life rooted in the close observance of religious strictures and values. The state also set up seminaries that trained state-appointed rabbis who would undermine the authority and power of established religious leaders selected by the Jewish community. Jewish youths—girls and boys—also attended privately financed schools that required the study of Russian and offered religious instruction and classes in Hebrew and secular subjects and handicrafts, which were viewed as productive and practical.

Jewish boys (and sometimes girls) attended a *kheyder* (or *heder*), which tended to be a poorly maintained room with a table surrounded by children, some as young as three or four, and employed inadequately trained teachers (*melamed*, singular) who focused solely on imparting elementary knowledge of Judaism by teaching boys and young men to read prayers in Hebrew (Figure 2.1). The following description by Lazar Gol'denberg, who became a revolutionary, provides insight into the life of a pupil in a *kheyder:*

> The children of ordinary Jews learned just enough about the mechanics of reading Hebrew to participate in religious life; hence most Jewish men lacked the literacy skills to comprehend any Hebrew texts beyond the rudimentary prayer book. Nor were all the long hours in the *heder* (from morning until evening) devoted to learning; most students also had to perform chores for the *melamed*'s wife or supervise other children.[10]

From the perspective of the government, the *kheyder* fostered religious fanaticism, hindered the ability and opportunity of Jews to

Figure 2.1 *Melamed* (teacher) and his pupils in a *kheyder*, 1920s
Courtesy of Blavatnik Archive Foundation (http://www.blavatnik.org)

integrate into Russian society, and did nothing to imbue students with the skills and knowledge to participate in secular, Russian society. As the memorandum written in the 1840s that served as the basis of the education reform put it, the "estrangement of the Jews from the general civil order" stemmed from the ideas of Judaism, which, read the memorandum, taught Jews that they were entitled to exploit Gentiles without any moral or ethical qualms. Policymakers believed they were engaged in a program of moral improvement through "the eradication of the superstitions and harmful prejudices instilled by the study of the Talmud."[11] The state also put schools run by the Jewish community and individuals and home tutoring under its watchful eye.

Given the goals of these new schools, why did the government, in paradoxical fashion, permit study of Judaic texts? It did so out of concern that Jews would not enroll their children in these schools if religious study was not permitted. The fact that Jewish parents tended to keep their boys from these schools out of fear that the government's real intent was to convert their children bore out the state's apprehension. While the vast majority of Jewish youths did not attend state-sponsored schools, some Jewish parents enrolled their boys in these schools, which gave rise to a generation of Jews who drew upon their secular education to become a small, but influential group of intellectuals who embraced progressive ideas and reforms and contributed to the transformation of Jewish culture. Many graduates of these schools became Russified, and many of these acculturated Jews fell into the orbit of radical ideas, joining one of the several revolutionary parties that emerged in Russia during the final decades of the nineteenth century. Of course, the fact that government efforts to divorce Jews from traditional values and institutions sometimes produced revolutionaries only confirmed the belief that Jews posed a fundamental threat to Russian society and culture. From the perspective of many Russian intellectuals and government policymakers, it made little difference if Jews were religious or secular.

The government's approach met with the ardent support of a small group of Jews who were inspired by the *Haskalah* in Central Europe. Known as *maskilim* (*maskil*, singular), they were proponents of Jewish integration and advocated the study of secular knowledge. They encouraged the adoption of values, attitudes, and behaviors that would reduce the social and cultural chasm between Jews and non-Jews. But they did not reject Judaism or even call for religious reform, as did many of their predecessors elsewhere on the continent. Still, they saw the value of not only learning Russian but also immersing themselves in secular subjects in order to prepare Russian Jewry for cultural and social transformation. Some also advocated learning Hebrew as a form of secular expression.

On the whole, the tsarist government under Nicholas I was unable to persuade many Jews to jettison traditional life and embrace the regime's efforts to bridge the gap between Jews and Russians. Jewish communities resented state interference in religious affairs, such as the appointment of rabbis, and felt similarly angry about other policies that chipped away at the community's autonomy to decide matters pertaining to religious and cultural concerns. Like the conscription of Jewish boys into military colonies and the subsequent pressure to convert, such policies did very little to endear the autocracy to Russian Jewry.

Tsar Alexander II (ruled 1855–81), who succeeded to the throne after Nicholas's death in 1855, pursued a host of policies designed to loosen the state's grip on his subjects and, as he understood it, modernize the empire. In doing so he turned his back on many of his father's strict conservative policies designed to protect the country from the supposedly subversive impact of West European intellectual, political, and socioeconomic trends that went hand in hand with the growth of liberalism, industrialization, urbanization, and socialism. Russia's humiliating defeat by England, France, and the Ottoman Empire in the Crimean War (1853–6) hammered home the message that the autocracy had to undertake reforms in order to compete militarily with its rivals and maintain its Great Power status. The new tsar launched a set of policies known as the Great Reforms that emancipated the peasantry from serfdom, reformed the judiciary and military, and established a system of limited local self-government. He also took initial steps to promote industrialization by developing the country's fledgling railway system and providing government contracts for industrial goods. The emancipation of the serfs would provide the basis of an industrial labor force since peasants, freed from the legal control of former serf owners, could seek employment in cities and factory towns if granted permission by their families and village.

Alexander II also made overtures to the Jewish community: he dismantled the military colonies, made it easier for Jews to attend universities and enter the civil service, and granted Jewish graduates of universities, along with wealthy merchants, army veterans, and certain artisans, the right to live outside the Pale of Settlement. Jews in tsarist Russia hoped that these measures were the prelude to the lifting of all legal and civil disabilities and the end of the Pale, thereby opening the empire's interior for Jewish settlement.[12] But the Tsar-Liberator, as Alexander II was known, rejected additional measures to ease the oppression of Jews. The refusal to end residency restrictions for the vast majority of Jews underscored how the tsarist government implemented policies that worked at cross-purposes. After all, how sincere could a government be that encouraged the integration of some Jews but maintained a bureaucratic edifice that ensured the overwhelming majority of Jews had to remain with the confines of the western borderlands of the empire? So long as Jews were restricted to life in the Pale, the prospects of the much-hoped for *sblizhenie*, or the coming together of Russian and Jews, were negligible. The reign of Alexander II's son, Tsar Alexander III (ruled 1881–94), made this abundantly clear.

Unlike his father, Tsar Alexander III walked back the state's conciliatory measures toward society in general and Jews in particular. Alexander III believed that Jews were responsible for the assassination of his father in 1881 by a group of revolutionaries (see Chapter 4). Whatever liberal tendencies came to the fore under Alexander II were quashed by his son who rejected progressive reforms of any kind, seeing them as contributing to political radicalism. Alexander III categorically rejected efforts to encourage the integration, no matter how limited, of Jews into gentile society. In his policies toward Jews, Alexander III imposed strict quotas (the *numerus clausus*) on the number of Jews who could attend universities and other schools of higher education. While Jewish enrollments in universities declined as a percentage, the absolute numbers of Jews attending university remained the same.[13]

In addition, the government, in 1882, enacted the Temporary Regulations, which were designed to prevent the movement of Jews into the countryside in the belief that this would reduce opportunities to exploit peasants. The Temporary Regulations, which remained on the books until 1917, prohibited new settlement of Jews outside the Pale, restricted the right of Jews to own and lease land outside the Pale's towns and cities, and prohibited Jews to conduct business on Sunday. Moreover, the government of Alexander III excluded Jews from serving on city councils, limited the number of Jews who could practice law, restricted opportunities for government employment, and at times expelled Jews from cities. For example, in 1891 the official in charge of Moscow ordered the expulsion of some 20,000 Jews from the city, notwithstanding the fact that many of them had earned the right to legally reside there. The last tsar of the Romanov dynasty, Nicholas II (ruled 1894–1917) hewed closely to the approach taken by his father, Alexander III, by maintaining a system of discriminatory policies toward Russia's Jews. He was a firm believer in the evil machinations of Jews and particularly blamed them for fomenting social unrest and political revolution. He was dead set against weakening the legal disabilities imposed on Russian Jewry and opposed any steps that would lead to its emancipation.

These measures to promote the acculturation and integration of Jews did little to alter the nature of Jewish society and culture. But other forces were at work that put in motion the gradual transformation of Russian Jewry.[14] By the end of the nineteenth century all of Russian society was in flux due to the combined impact of urbanization, industrialization, increasing literacy rates, and the breakdown of the system of legal estates (*sosloviia*). Not surprisingly, the Jewish community also experienced change, notwithstanding the Jews' resistance to state-inspired programs to promote assimilation. Jewry in tsarist Russia was not homogenous, and many Jews underwent a transformation over the course of the late nineteenth century, which belies the commonplace belief that all Jews were intent on maintaining their distance from the Russian mainstream.

By 1900 many Jews were embarking on paths that brought them into closer contact with Russian society and culture. Exposure to secular education served to alienate many Jews from their religious parents and contributed to their political radicalization. Their ties to Judaism, particularly what we today would label "Ultra-Orthodox" and traditional Jewish life, grew attenuated as more and more Russian Jews gravitated to Russian culture and society, and took advantage of the offerings of urban life. Acculturated Jews adopted Western-styled dress; men shaved their beards and sidelocks; women stopped covering their heads, legs, and arms in public; and more and more Jews learned Russian, stopped attending synagogue, socialized with non-Jews, and moved in social circles outside their formerly circumscribed realm. Jewish society in late Imperial Russia was a world in flux. Like most— Jewish and Gentile—communities at that time, Jewish society was not free of conflict: tensions and resentments rooted in socioeconomic grievances, the exercise of communal power and authority, religious differences, and generational antagonism characterized relationships among Russian Jews no matter where they lived. In the city of Odesa, with the empire's fourth largest number of inhabitants (35 percent of whom were Jews) and home to the country's major port, disagreement and discord pitted Jews intent on reforming the practice and observance of Judaism with religious traditionalists. So-called modern Jews, many of whom were young adults intent on acculturating into gentile society, displayed their contempt and disregard for their pious parents and grandparents by flouting social and religious conventions such as not fasting on Yom Kippur, attending classes on the Sabbath if they were enrolled in secular schools, and partying on the High Holidays.[15]

Thousands of Russian Jews chose to convert to Orthodoxy and other Christian denominations.[16] Jews seeking to convert had to petition church authorities for permission. The following petition by Freida Poliakova, a Jewish woman from the Lithuanian town of Kovno, underscores the sincerity and fervor of these converts. In 1866 she wrote to the Bishop of Kovno for Baptism:

> For a long time, I have nourished a desire to embrace Christianity. I fully understand that the promised Messiah in the Old Testament—Jesus Christ—has already come and is revered among Christians. I believe in him with all my heart and soul and can no longer remain in Judaism, …
>
> With these feelings and the recognition of the above-stated truths, I left my husband in Minsk and arrived here [in Kovno] in order to realize my wish, at least without any impediments …. My daughter Mariia (known as Merka in Judaism), who is seven years old, is with me. My daughter and I are already preparing to receive the saving baptism of the Russian Orthodox faith because we have studied all the principles of the Christian faith, life, and prayers for a long time by ourselves.

The bishop approved Poliakova's petition.[17]

The following photographs illustrate the coexistence of the modern and secular and the traditional and religious ways of life of

Russian Jews at the turn of the twentieth century. Figure 2.2 shows a grandfather at prayer (note the prayer shawl and phylacteries) standing next to his granddaughter, identified as a radical student, who is dressed in modern garb and not covering her hair. Figure 2.3 is a postcard of two Jews greeting each other on Rosh Hashanah, the Jewish New Year, probably in the early twentieth century. The man on the left is a Reform Jew dressed in Western-styled clothes, while the one on the right is an Orthodox Jew wearing traditional religious clothing. Despite the differences in their attachment to traditional

Figure 2.2 Grandfather and granddaughter, early twentieth century
Courtesy of YIVO Institute for Jewish Research

Figure 2.3 Postcard of a secular and religious Jew, date unknown
Courtesy of YIVO Institute for Jewish Research

Judaism, both observe one of the most important religious holidays for Jews. The caption reads:

"Reform or Hasid,
Rich or Poor.

Figure 2.4 A Hasidic rebbe on a walk with his followers, 1924
Courtesy of YIVO Institute for Jewish Research

Press Hands, Brothers, Happy New Year
Whoever or Whatever You are!"

Figure 2.4 is a photograph (1924) of a Hasidic rebbe on a walk with his followers who have beards and are wearing black caftans and hats or other head coverings. Hasidism was a religious movement that emerged in the mid-eighteenth century in opposition to traditional Jewish life centered on rabbis and synagogues. The movement centered around charismatic *tsadikim* (enlightened ones) who emphasized mystical teachings and the joy of prayer rather than the study of the Torah and Talmud. The final photograph (Figure 2.5) is that of Rabbi Moses Etter, the author's grandfather. Born in Lithuania, Rabbi Etter took over the rabbinical post of his father-in-law in Chechersk, Belarus, a town of several thousand inhabitants. Even though he attended an Orthodox rabbinical seminary, Rabbi Etter found himself as head of a congregation of Hasidim in Chechersk. After he emigrated to Harrisburg, Pennsylvania, with his family in the mid-1920s, Rabbi

Figure 2.5 Rabbi Moses Etter (1883–1966), the author's grandfather. Prior to emigrating to Harrisburg, Pennsylvania, in the mid-1920s, Rabbi Etter led a congregation of Hasidim in Chechersk, a town of several thousand inhabitants in Belarus

Personal Collection of Author

Etter became the rabbi of an Orthodox congregation for the next several decades.

Despite the shifts in the lifestyles, values, and behaviors of many Jewish men and women and the attenuation of their ties to traditional Jewish society and Judaism, the overwhelming majority of Jews in the Russian Empire remained firmly rooted in the world of tradition that revolved around the daily rhythms governed by the dictates of Judaism. It took the tectonic shifts brought about by the Bolshevik Revolution to trigger a massive change in how Russian Jews lived. The collapse of the autocracy in early 1917 and the consolidation of communist rule under the leadership of Vladimir Lenin led to the abolition of the Pale of Settlement and the end to all laws that restricted the ability of Jews to integrate into Russian society. Similar to the approach taken by the tsars, the new rulers of Russia combined both carrot and stick in their policies toward the Jewish minority, whose numbers had halved (from nearly 5.5 million in 1914 to 2.6 million by 1926) due to immigration, the impact of seven years of war, and the loss of territory due to the emergence of Poland and Lithuania as independent states after the end of the First World War. The vast majority of Jews living under communist rule after 1917 did not embrace Marxism, but most Soviet Jews welcomed the new government's policies that actively combated antisemitism and lifted all limitations on where Jews could live and what kind of work they could pursue. Soviet power contributed to the transformation of Jewish culture and society.

By the 1920s many shtetl and small-town Jews, particularly young men and women, jumped at the promise of new lives afforded by the regime's effort to promote social mobility and integration. They poured into the cities of European Russia to escape the dead-end life of impoverished shtetls, where unemployment reached crisis proportions in the 1920s, and they took advantage of educational and economic opportunities that had been denied them under the tsars. These developments continued to grow apace once the Kremlin under Stalin's direction embarked on a concerted plan to transform all aspects of society in the 1930s through rapid industrialization, urbanization, and the brutal suppression of private economic life. Not surprisingly, one result was increased secularization of the younger generation of Jews who broke free of the religious and cultural traditions of their families and immersed themselves in efforts to build a society dedicated to socialism and militant atheism.

The regime's effort to promote the building of a socialist Jewish culture and society rooted in Yiddish paradoxically led to its disappearance as the lingua franca of Soviet Jews. Despite state support in the 1920s and 1930s for elementary and some high schools where Yiddish was the language of instruction, many Jewish parents resisted enrolling their children in them because they lacked meaningful Jewish content and could lead Jewish youths away from traditional culture. Moreover, many young Jews realized that opportunities to get ahead in Soviet society were limited if they did not learn Russian, which they viewed as the gateway to social mobility. After all, avenues of advancement were limited, if not nonexistent, for Yiddish speakers once they sought to continue their secondary and higher education and embark on careers. Even if they used Yiddish at work, they also would need to be fluent in Russian so they could be on equal footing with non-Yiddish speakers. As more and more Jewish youths learned Russian, the need for Yiddish newspapers, journals, and books correspondingly decreased. To be sure, most Jews who had come of age prior to 1917 remained traditional in their lifestyles and commitment to a religious way of life. But their children and grandchildren read the writing on the wall and chose to integrate and acculturate. One telling sign of traditional Jewish society's increasing obsolescence was the fact that by 1939, 40 percent of Jews who had been living in the former Pale of Settlement had moved elsewhere in the Soviet Union, where life and conventions tended to be secular and Russified.[18] The Nazi genocide of Yiddish-speaking Jews living in the territory of the former Pale of Settlement was the final nail in the coffin of traditional shtetl life.

Another indicator of this growing social and cultural integration was the higher rate of intermarriage between Jews and non-Jews. Intermarriage was rare among Russian Jews prior to the revolution, but by 1936, 20 percent of Jewish men and 18 percent of Jewish women married non-Jews, a clear sign of the integrationist desires of Soviet Jews. By 1988 the rate of intermarriage had grown to 62.5 percent for men and 52 percent for women. Yet another marker of the collapse of ethnic barriers was the disappearance of Yiddish as the primary language of Jews. By 1939 41.5 percent of Jews in the Soviet Union claimed Yiddish as their native language, far below the 98 percent of Jews living in the Pale of Settlement in the 1890s. And the number of Yiddish speakers continued to decline in the following decades. By the time the Soviet Union collapsed in 1991, the percentage had dropped to under 15 percent.[19]

The state's coercive policies reinforced this process of integration and assimilation. As we learned in Chapter 1, the Kremlin's assault on Judaism and its institutions meant that Jews coming of age during the initial decades of communist rule risked the wrath of the state if they pursued a religious way of life. Furthermore, the closing of *kheyders*, yeshivas, and rabbinical seminaries and the prohibition of the publication of books, particularly prayer books, in Hebrew, made it difficult for Jews to preserve their traditional way of life and hindered their ability to maintain the link between Jewish society and Judaism, especially among the younger generation.

Leading the way in the campaign were the Jewish Sections of the Communist Party (*evsektsiia*), which agitated and propagandized among Soviet Jews, exhorting them to embrace the values of the proletarian revolution. Not only did the Jewish Sections lead the campaign to root out Judaism and religious observance among Jews, but they spearheaded efforts to suppress Hebrew culture and Zionist and non-Bolshevik affiliations. In the 1920s and 1930s book publishing and theater, especially in Yiddish, thrived as the government funded the arts so long as journalists, novelists, and playwrights promoted the building of socialism to the detriment of traditional religious culture and Zionism. The Moscow State Yiddish Theater, for example, was regarded as one of the best theaters in the Soviet Union in the two decades after the establishment of communist power, and it trained men and women to perform in Yiddish theater troupes throughout the country. Its avant-garde productions promoted the goals of Soviet communism and garnered accolades from theater critics in both the Soviet Union and abroad, especially after its European tour in 1928.[20]

Figure 2.6 Scene from *Kheyder*, an antireligious play, 1920s. The letters on the rears of the actors spell "Kosher"

Courtesy of YIVO Institute for Jewish Research

The Kremlin dismantled the Jewish Sections in 1930, but the government's pressure on traditional Jewish life and institutions did not abate. As we shall see in Chapter 4, government policies by the late 1940s revived this onslaught on any expression of Jewish identity and culture that did not hew closely to the dictates of the Kremlin. The Moscow State Yiddish Theater shut its doors in 1949, and the government closed other Yiddish cultural institutions. Finally, the Holocaust also contributed to the death knell of traditional Jewish culture and society. The territory conquered by Germany coincided with areas with the greatest concentration of Jews: over two million Jews living on Soviet territory were murdered by the Germans and their Polish, Ukrainian, Latvian, and Lithuanian accomplices, thereby destroying the foundation of traditional Jewish life and culture in the Soviet Union. Shtetl life, which was already dying out by the end of the 1930s due to social, economic, and political transformation, vanished completely as a result of the genocide of the Jews.

***

Over the course of the twentieth century Russian Jews assimilated and integrated into Russian society and culture: their attachment to Judaism grew tenuous, indeed almost wholly nonexistent, and they became highly Russified. They identified more with the poems of Alexander Pushkin, the founder of modern Russian literature, than with the stories of Sholem Aleichem who captured, in Yiddish, the daily life of shtetl Jews. In the words of one historian, "college educated Soviets," which included Jews, "lived with Pushkin, Herzen, Tolstoy, and Chekhov" and "the leap into socialism resulted in Russification."[21] Soviet Jews acquired a hybrid ethno-cultural identity, one that saw them identify as Soviet and Jewish, or in the words of one scholar "Soviet and kosher," notwithstanding the fact that most knew next to nothing about Judaism's strictures about food except for the prohibition on eating pork.[22] Jewishness became, in other words, a "symbolic ethnicity."[23] Nevertheless, no amount of secularization and acculturation safeguarded them from accusations that they were outsiders who did not embrace mainstream culture and values and stubbornly resisted blending into the gentile world. The persistence of official and popular antisemitism, particularly after the Second World War, helped keep alive Jewish identity. The next two chapters underscore the persistence of the Jewish question: just as Jews were viewed as a minority people whose religious heritage and culture prevented their integration into Russian society, so too did the perception that they posed a threat because of their socioeconomic profile and political allegiances. Even though the bases of the Jewish question weakened, Jews still fell victim to accusations that they endangered the well-being and stability of the country.

CHAPTER 3
THE SOCIOECONOMIC QUESTION: LAND AND LABOR

For centuries Christians have accused Jews of exploiting Gentiles as merchants, shopkeepers, moneylenders, and petty traders. Judaism in the minds of many non-Jews celebrated crass materialism, which purportedly lay at the heart of many of the values, attitudes, and behaviors of Jews that comprised the Jewish question. Jewish religious texts gave rise to spurious accusations that have persisted for two millennia and still animate antisemitic attacks in the twenty-first century. For many Christians the source of Jewish exploitation can be traced to the Hebrew Scriptures, which purportedly valued the accumulation of wealth. Deuteronomy 23:21, in particular, sanctioned the lending of money with interest to foreigners, that is, to non-Jews. Even though most Jewish rabbinic scholars reject this view, the belief that Judaic strictures authorized the economic exploitation of non-Jews by Jews became firmly planted in the popular mindset of Christians and became a hallmark of antisemitic thought and practice.[1]

Prohibited from owning land and becoming artisans throughout Europe since the Middle Ages, Jews gravitated toward occupations that filled valuable niches in the agrarian economy of Europe, particularly Eastern Europe, well into the nineteenth century. In the territory that became part of the Russian Empire in the late eighteenth century, the majority of Jews lived in small market towns that dotted the countryside. Some Jews worked as managers of estates, tax collectors, and middlemen who facilitated the exchange of goods between country and city. Others owned small shops; engaged in small-scale handicraft production as tailors, shoemakers, and makers of leather goods that did not require them to take a Christian oath; produced and marketed dairy products; and peddled goods in the countryside. In addition, many Jews possessed leases to operate taverns and sell alcohol to villagers, which, according to tsarist officials, siphoned away the peasants' money, undermined their sobriety, and left them indebted to Jews who resorted to exploitative business practices such as price-gouging. A century later, according to the 1897 census, Jews were still overwhelmingly concentrated in commerce, retail trade, and small-scale manufacturing. Approximately 70 percent of Jews who reported the source of their income worked producing clothes and shoes in small enterprises and engaged in commercial activity of some sort. They had also made inroads into certain professions such as law, medicine, and journalism, and a very small number had joined the ranks of the wealthy as bankers, financiers, and owners of large import-export firms and food processing plants. Operating brothels was one trade open to Jewish women, who comprised 24 percent of madams in the empire in the late nineteenth century. Moreover, Jewish women owned 70 percent of brothels in the Pale at the turn of the twentieth century.[2]

The vast majority of non-Jews toiled as peasants, who made up over 90 percent of the populace of the empire and, according to officials who studied the Jewish question, resented the Jews' supposed control of the local economy. Policymakers viewed Jews as parasites who thrived on the exploitation of defenseless peasants who had been enserfed until 1861. As Count Nikolai Ignat'ev, minister of interior, noted in his explanation of why peasants attacked Jews and their property in 1881 after the assassination of Tsar Alexander II:

The main reason for behavior so uncharacteristic of Russians lies in circumstances of an exclusively economic kind. In the last twenty years the Jews, little by little, have taken over not only trade and production … all but a few of them have bent every effort to not increase the productive forces of the country but to exploit the native inhabitants, and primarily the poorer classes. This provoked the protest of the latter.[3]

The following drawing (Figure 3.1), which appeared in the right-wing newspaper *Veche* (The Realm) in 1906, offers a visual depiction

Figure 3.1 A Jew squeezing a Russian

Veche (The Realm), no. 79 (October 26, 1906). Courtesy of The Bridge Research Network

of purported Jewish exploitation. In the drawing a male Jew with stereotypical facial features such as a large hooked nose, thick lips, and sidelocks is shown squeezing a Russian in a giant vise. Beads of sweat drip down the victim's forehead, and blood oozes from his fingertips, a not very subtle allusion to the perceived domination and oppression of Russians by Jews.

As the Russian economy developed over the course of the nineteenth century, the accusation that Jewish bankers and financiers were conspiring to dominate gentile society by amassing wealth and controlling the workings of global capitalism became another integral characteristic of the Jewish question both inside and outside the Russian Empire. The canard that Jews engaged in unfair business practices and exploited gentile society economically dated back centuries. But it gained currency by the turn of the twentieth century as an intrinsic part of the belief that Jews were engaged in an organized and deliberate plot, devised by rabbis and the wealthy leaders of the community, to subvert gentile society and ensure Jewish control of the levers of economic and political power. Jewish capitalists allegedly manipulated stock markets, fixed prices, and loaned money at usurious rates in order to enhance their economic clout, bankrupt non-Jewish businesses, and make governments dependent on "Jewish" money. In an 1877 antisemitic screed, the Russian writer Fyodor Dostoevsky accused Jews of possessing a "thirst for our sweat and blood … Jews reign over all the stock exchanges … control credit … and control the whole of international politics." According to Dostoevsky, Jews also sought "a stronger and surer hold over humanity" in an effort to "mold the world" according to their "image and … essence."[4]

With the vast interior of the empire largely off-limits to them, Russian Jews lacked the opportunity to move around the empire in search of work and fill economic niches in cities, towns, and the countryside. While many Jews migrated to large towns and cities within the Pale of Settlement, life in major urban centers did not remedy the situation since population pressures continued to grow and intensified competition among Jews and between Jews and non-Jews. Straitened economic circumstances forced more Jews into greater poverty. Life in the Pale also maintained existing social and economic relations between peasants and Jews, which contributed to the continuation of tensions, resentments, bad blood, and prejudice. Competition among Jews and between Gentiles and Jews to earn livings as shopkeepers and handicraft workers also intensified.

Limited geographic mobility prevented the siphoning of excess Jewish labor to markets that needed handicraft workshops and retail stores. The only outlet for the burgeoning Jewish population was emigration to countries in Western Europe and Central Europe and North America, primarily the United States. Over the course of the nineteenth century, Russian Jewry experienced growing impoverishment, which prompted over two million Jews to seek better lives elsewhere between 1880 and 1914.

One tactic tsarist officials adopted to combat supposed Jewish economic exploitation took its inspiration from ideas and policies developed in Western Europe. Like other efforts to reform the Jews' way of life, officials formulated policies to transform the socioeconomic makeup of Jewish society. In the eighteenth century the notion that land and agriculture were the source of a society's wealth (known as physiocracy) dominated the thinking of many intellectuals and officials particularly in France but elsewhere in Europe as well. Jews were perceived as engaged in non-productive labor: they were said to avoid physical work, make money without producing anything tangible, and exploit peasants by controlling commerce and owning shops. In the 1780s, for example, Emperor Joseph II of the Habsburg Monarchy engaged in an early form of social engineering by issuing an edict that encouraged Jews to move to the land. According to this thinking, settling Jews on the land would "normalize" the socioeconomic profile of Jewry, reduce the exploitation of non-Jews, allow Jews to demonstrate their willingness to fit into gentile society, and promote the integration of Jews into mainstream society.

Tsar Alexander I followed suit when, in 1804, he enacted a statute that encouraged the settlement of Jews on the land through agricultural colonization. He set aside land in New Russia, territory in southern Ukraine near the Black Sea that had been incorporated into the empire in the late 1700s, for purchase by Jews. But Jews were wary of uprooting themselves to take a chance as farmers, a way of life with which they had virtually no experience and little respect, regarding it as an uncultured pursuit. Jews were also concerned that they would be cut off from religious and other communal institutions such as schools, burial societies, and social welfare programs. The project also foundered because the law, following in the footsteps of other tsarist policies regarding Jews, worked at cross-purposes with other legislation. At the same time that Alexander encouraged Jews to farm as agricultural colonists, the 1804 statute also restricted Jews from renting land and ordered them to leave the countryside. For the remainder of the nineteenth century tsarist authorities worked to limit the presence of Jews in rural Russia in order to protect the peasantry. But they never abandoned the resettlement program, though the state did not devote the resources needed to lure Jews to the land. By the turn of the twentieth century approximately 200,000 Jews (a drop in the bucket considering that over 5 million Jews lived in the Russian Empire) were engaged in farming. Clearly, the effort to transform the occupational profile of Russian Jewry fell way short of the government's goals.

The communist government that came to power in 1917 shared the same views with its tsarist predecessors regarding the need to alter the occupational profile of Jews. From the outset the Bolsheviks ensured Jews full rights of citizenship and pursued a policy to stamp out antisemitism. But concern about Jewish exploitation of non-Jews remained a focus of Bolshevik policy during the first two decades of communist rule. In this respect the year 1917 is less important than one would assume since both tsarist and communist administrators shared similar views toward the occupational profile of Jews and worried about Jews taking advantage of peasants. Even more than the tsarist regime, the communists ruling in the Kremlin were intent on transforming the socioeconomic profile of Soviet Jews by eliminating occupations deemed capitalist and petty bourgeois, and therefore exploitative.

The promise of building a socialist society prompted Soviet officials in the decade after the revolution to make it difficult for Jews engaged in commerce (even those who owned small shops or were poor, itinerant traders) to make a living. Jews in these occupations were stripped of the right to vote and were subjected to other discriminatory policies that made it difficult to stay in business.[5] The Kremlin implemented these policies even though government policy in the 1920s known as the New Economic Policy tolerated private enterprise and trade. This government campaign against Jews who worked in commerce and retail trade also encompassed handicraft workers who, notwithstanding their involvement in manual, productive labor, were targeted because they owned or worked in private workshops. According to the 1926 census, just under 28 percent of Jews of working age in the Soviet Union were classified as artisans, or persons engaged in handicraft production of clothing, leather goods, and foodstuffs. Another 12 percent worked in factories, while approximately 24 percent were engaged in non-manual work (either as owners or employees) such as the service sector, retail trade, office work, and the professions such as medicine, law, and education.[6] Higher rates of taxation and difficulties obtaining raw materials and equipment and marketing goods—the result of deliberate government policy—were part of the Kremlin's plan to weaken private production and trade in the 1920s. One consequence was the increased impoverishment of shtetl Jews who found it hard to make ends meet as they were squeezed out of the economy. In the late 1920s the Communist Party's decision to outlaw private trade and enterprise as part of its wholesale drive to industrialize the country through state control of the economy spelled the end of small-scale manufacturing that provided livelihoods for many Jews.

This effort to engineer a new Jewish society led the authorities to continue the tsarist emphasis on productivization, especially in terms of turning displaced Jewish shopkeepers, petty traders, and unskilled workers into toilers on the land and in large-scale industry who would find their electoral rights restored. Not only was this ideologically desirable from the perspective of the Kremlin, but officials hoped that this policy would enable Jews to escape the grinding poverty of life in the former Pale of Settlement. The solution to the Jewish question, under both tsarism and communism, depended on transforming Jews from what was perceived as a harmful and retrograde community to one incapable of causing social and economic damage. In many respects, the approach adopted by the Kremlin in the 1920s resembled the thinking of Zionist[7] activists who established *kibbutzim* (agricultural communes) in the Land of Israel beginning in the late nineteenth century.

The following poster (Figure 3.2), published in the early 1920s, illustrates the communist regime's desire to remake the socioeconomic profile of Soviet Jews. The employment of Yiddish underscores the government's desire to deliver its message to as many Jews as possible in the language that was deemed the mother tongue of Soviet Jews. The text in the middle of the poster reads: "The old school produced slaves; the Soviet school prepares healthy, skilled workers who are builders

Figure 3.2 "The old school produced slaves; the Soviet school prepares healthy, skilled workers" (1920)

Courtesy of The Magnes Collection of Jewish Art and Life, UC Berkeley.

of the socialist order. The *kheyder* leads to the shop, synagogue, and enmity among peoples. The Soviet school leads to the factory, land, and unity among peoples." The images on the left illustrate how religious observance and the traditional one-room primary school and petit-bourgeois commerce led to undesirable consequences; the images on the right depict how Soviet power, with its emphasis on secular education, would give rise to modern agriculture and factory work, and promote good will and mutual trust among citizens. In other words, the Kremlin predicated its approach to Jews on the belief that traditional Jewish life fostered values and behaviors antithetical to the socialist ethos under construction during the early years of the Soviet Union.

In the 1920s and 1930s the Kremlin pursued a policy that encouraged the agricultural settlement of Jews. The publication of the journal *The Jewish Peasant* (Evreiskii krestianin), which appeared in Yiddish and Russian in the mid-1920s, was one sign of the Kremlin's commitment to productivization, particularly the desire to agrarianize Jews as productive toilers on the land. The cover of issue 2 (Figure 3.3) shows a Jewish farmer tilling the land with a tractor, a sign of modernization that the regime hoped would make inroads into traditional peasant agriculture.

In addition, the government set aside land in southern Ukraine, Belarus, Crimea, and the Soviet Far East and recruited Jews hoping to start new lives far from what was perceived as the dead-end world of shtetl life. The government also allocated land to Jews in parts of the Caucasus and Uzbekistan. Early discussions focused on setting a target of 500,000 Jewish agricultural colonists, and the government established two organizations, the state-run KOMZET (Committee for the Settlement of Jewish Toilers on the Land) and OZET (Society for the Settlement of Jewish Toilers on the Land). The latter was, in principle, a non-governmental organization, but in reality it found itself working at the behest of the Kremlin to promote land colonization. It also entered into contracts with several foreign Jewish philanthropies to provide material support such as farm equipment, housing, loans, and training. By the eve of the Second World War, a few hundred thousand Jews had settled on the land, with many colonies in Crimea prospering. While falling short of the original goal of half a million, the program provided new opportunities for tens of thousands of Soviet Jews and, if not for the invasion by Germany in 1941 and the devastation caused by the war and genocide, it is possible that many of these settlements would have continued to flourish.[8]

Figure 3.3 The cover of *The Jewish Peasant* (Evreiskii krestianin)

The Jewish Peasant, no. 2 (1926). Digital Image © The Museum of Modern Art/Licensed by SCALA / Art Resource, New York

Figure 3.4, a poster issued in 1932, exhorts members of OZET to "help transform Jewish toilers into active builders of a socialist society" and illustrates the Kremlin's efforts to publicize for the Soviet and non-Soviet public the government's commitment to promoting Jewish agricultural settlement. In contrast to the tractor driver depicted on the cover of *The Jewish Peasant*, the Jewish women and men portrayed in this poster rely on hoes and a horse-drawn wagon, a clear indicator that the hoped-for mechanization of farming had not yet been realized.

Lastly, Figure 3.5 illustrates the Soviet effort to create a new Jewish man and woman who embraced the secular ethos of socialism and rejected both Judaism and capitalism. The breeding of oversized pigs, a taboo food for religious Jews, alluded to the secularization of Jews under communism and publicized the extent to which many Jews had left behind dietary strictures such as the eating of pork.[9] The poster, produced in 1931, proclaims at the top in Yiddish that "The pig is our main machine for the production of meat in the near future," while the text at the bottom demands the organization of "Agricultural councils and collective farms to raise pigs." In the background are the houses of collective farmers who raise the pigs in what appear to be modern facilities, evidence of the supposed material prosperity of Jews engaged in animal husbandry.

The Kremlin also devoted enormous attention and resources to settling Jews in the Jewish Autonomous Region (JAR), a territory located some five thousand miles from Moscow along the border with China and popularly known as Birobidzhan, the region's capital city (see Map 3.1).[10] The idea of establishing the JAR stemmed from the government's nationality policy of the 1920s and 1930s. The architects of the Soviet Union's approach to nationality, primarily Vladimir Lenin and Joseph Stalin, believed that land, labor, and language were the essential elements of the country's ethno-national minorities, which numbered over one hundred. Each ethnic and national minority merited its own territory that would be the locus of the building of socialism according to the dictum "national in form, socialist in content." In the case of Birobidzhan, Jews would engage in productive labor, specifically agriculture, and develop cultural institutions based

Figure 3.4 "Help transform Jewish toilers into active builders of a socialist society" (1932)

Courtesy of Blavatnik Archive Foundation (http://www.blavatnik.org), https://www.blavatnikarchive.org/manifest/mv?manifest=22962

Figure 3.5 "The pig is our main machine for the production of meat in the near future" (1931)

Courtesy of Blavatnik Archive Foundation (http://www.blavatnik.org), https://www.blavatnikarchive.org/manifest/mv?manifest=22965

on Yiddish and socialist principles, which were dictated by the central authorities. Moreover, the architects of Birobidzhan believed its existence would weaken the appeal of Zionism and some Jews' commitment to establishing a Jewish state in the Land of Israel.

Beginning in 1924, officials began searching for a territory that could serve as a base for Jewish agricultural settlement and the nucleus of a national homeland. In 1928 the Kremlin designated a region the size of Belgium along the China–Soviet border as the official national center of Soviet Jewry. Many prominent Jewish government and party officials voiced their opposition to creating a Jewish homeland thousands of miles from where most Soviet Jews lived. But in the end Stalin endorsed the settlement of Jews in what would become known as Birobidzhan and, after 1934, the Jewish Autonomous Region.

The decision to establish the JAR testified to the commitment by Soviet authorities to transform the socioeconomic profile of Jews. In particular, the government targeted unemployed and unskilled

Map 3.1 Map of Soviet Union with location of the Jewish Autonomous Region (Birobidzhan)

Courtesy of Bill Nelson Maps

workers who had little opportunity to find employment in factories, and would embrace life on the land as a way to leave behind the poverty of shtetl life. One advantage of Birobidzhan, in the eyes of the Kremlin, was the absence of a sizable indigenous population that would protest the allocation of land to Jewish interlopers. Another was its location along the border with China in a relatively underpopulated region rich with untapped economic resources and possessing geostrategic significance to counter Japanese expansionism.

Even though the overwhelming majority of Soviet Jews lived thousands of miles to the west of Birobidzhan and had no farming experience, the government believed that Birobidzhan was an attractive region for the experiment in transforming Jews into productive citizens who contributed to the building of socialism. Despite the fact that an economic infrastructure was not in place and the land, marshy and in need of drainage, was inhospitable, the proponents of Birobidzhan went full steam ahead recruiting settlers. Nor did the fact that Jews were wary of moving thousands of miles to somewhere cold, unfamiliar, and remote deter Moscow authorities from pursuing their plan to turn Birobidzhan into the center of Soviet Jewish culture and life.

The regime publicized the benefits and promise of Birobidzhan, which excited those Soviet Jews committed to the socialist experiment. In 1926 Mikhail Kalinin, president of the Soviet Union, expressed hope that Birobidzhan would facilitate the transformation of Soviet Jewry into "an economically stable, agriculturally compact group."[11] Semen Dimanshtein, the party official in charge of Jewish affairs, noted that populating Birobidzhan with Jews would "strengthen the tempo of the productivization of the Jewish poor.[12] Other advocates of Jewish agricultural resettlement believed that Birobidzhan would bring about the rejuvenation of Soviet Jewry.

What motivated Jews to move to Birobidzhan, and why did the Soviet government, which provided discounted train tickets and food subsidies for the journey, and housing and land once they arrived, send them there? One of the first Jews to move to the region proclaimed, "I thank you, comrades, for sending me here. Here I am getting settled and will stop living life like a 'Jew,' that is as a *luftmensch.*" Luftmensch is a Yiddish word that means "person of air," that is, someone without a definite occupation and skills and therefore lives on nothing. In 1928 a young Jewish man arrived in Birobidzhan and proclaimed that he had moved from the western region of the Soviet Union so he could become "a peasant." Another Jewish man concurred, noting that he did not want the life of a "small shopkeeper."[13] Neither man had any prior experience with farming. And yet they now found themselves far from friends and family in a remote area of the Soviet Far East where they hoped to refashion themselves as farmers. Figure 3.6 is a photograph of members of the ICOR commune in 1930, which was home to many foreign Jews who had settled in Birobidzhan. Figure 3.7 shows members of the ICOR commune posing while plowing a field.

Figure 3.8 celebrates the effort to "transform the Jewish Autonomous Region into the flowering" area of the Soviet Far East. The photo montage from 1936 depicts smiling, contented inhabitants of Birobidzhan—young and old, men and women—engaged in a variety of work and leisure activities, along with the achievements of the building of

Figure 3.6 Members of ICOR commune in 1930, which was home to many foreign Jews

Courtesy of Library of Congress. *Kommuna "Ikor" molodezhnaia. Na senokose u reki Tunguski 6/7g.* Russian Federation Jewish Autonomous Oblast Birobidzhan, 1930. [Place of Publication Not Identified: Publisher Not Identified] Photograph. https://www.loc.gov/item/2018683001/

socialism. Not surprisingly, the one adult woman shown is taking care of her baby, a tell-tale sign of the persistence of traditional gender roles that coexisted with the regime's emphasis on women's participation in the paid workforce. Also included is an excerpt from comments made by Joseph Stalin praising the socialist experiment. Unlike the previous images, Figure 3.8 depicts the emergence of a society filled with an infrastructure of tractors, buses, and apartment complexes under development. It also shows a generation of young Soviet citizens whose smiles suggest their satisfaction with the socialist way of life.

The designation of Birobidzhan as a region reserved for the settlement of only Jews, however, was honored more in the breach than in reality. Jewish settlement in Birobidzhan began in earnest

Figure 3.7 Members of ICOR commune in 1930
Personal Collection of Author

in mid-1928, and by the end of the 1930s, some 18,000 Jews had migrated to the region that was home to nearly 110,000 people, Jew and non-Jew alike. Of those Jews engaged in agriculture, they toiled on collective farms, not on their own land. Most Jews who did move to Birobidzhan shied away from agriculture, preferring to work in stores, offices, and factories that emerged as the Soviet Union launched its rapid industrialization and urbanization drives in the late 1920s at the same time as it committed resources to settling Jews on the land. It is not difficult to imagine that the novel and challenging life as a "peasant" did not appeal to many Jews, who lacked farming experience and know-how. Furthermore, not long after creating the Soviet Jewish homeland, the Kremlin abandoned efforts to agrarianize Jews, choosing instead to recruit Jews into factories, workshops, stores, and offices.

In addition, Jews living in the western borderlands of the Soviet Union hesitated to uproot themselves and families to make the daunting trip of thousands of miles to settle in an unfamiliar region far from established Jewish life and culture. Most preferred to leave

Figure 3.8 "Let's transform the Jewish Autonomous Region into the flowering region of the Far Eastern District" (1936)

Courtesy of Blavatnik Archive Foundation (http://www.blavatnik.org), https://www.blavatnikarchive.org/manifest/mv?manifest=22966

their hometowns for urban centers such as Moscow, Minsk, Odessa, Kyiv, and Leningrad, where work and educational opportunities abounded. Those Jews who did move to Birobidzhan found living and working conditions that were far from satisfactory, prompting many of them to return home or move to more established towns and cities in the Soviet Far East.[14] The plan to populate Birobidzhan with large numbers of Jews came to naught by the end of the 1930s.

***

Efforts to transform the occupational profile of Russian and Soviet Jewry via settlement on the land did not have much success. But the promotion of Jewish agricultural settlement highlights the fact that both tsarist and communist officials worried about the supposed deleterious economic impact Jews had on non-Jewish society. In other words, 1917, the year that marked a new political beginning for Russia, did not alter persistent attitudes shared by governments both before and after the collapse of tsardom with regard to Jewish economic pursuits. Indeed, these prejudices remained long after the communists had seized control and set out to transform society. In the late 1950s Nikita Khrushchev, who succeeded Stalin as leader of the Soviet Union, responded to a journalist's query about the status of Birobidzhan with the comment that Birobidzhan had failed to turn Soviet Jews into agricultural workers because:

> Jews have always preferred the trades of craftsmen: they are tailors, they work with glass or precious stones, they are businessmen, pharmacists, frequently carpenters. But, if you take building or metallurgy—mass professions—you might not, to my knowledge, come across a single Jew there. They do not like collective work, group discipline. They have always preferred to be dispersed. They are individualists.[15]

He also noted that Jews tended to pursue intellectual endeavors, which implied that physical labor did not attract them. In other words, Jews did not, and could not, participate in the building of socialism as manual workers.

Another indicator that the government continued to believe that Jews were still attracted to occupations such as the retail and service sectors, which were prone to corrupt business practices, was a series of trials in the early and mid-1960s. The Kremlin held hundreds of trials of Soviet citizens accused of a variety of economic crimes such as embezzlement, bribery, and currency speculation. The press publicized those defendants with Jewish-sounding names, which drew upon official and popular prejudices toward Jews as economic exploiters. The fact that the Kremlin meted out harsher penalties, including the death sentence, to Jews than to non-Jews indicates that regime still believed that Jews, who tended to work in non-manual work in the service sector, retail trade, and white-collar sectors, were a political liability.

The fact that Jews did not turn into farmers does not mean, however, that the socioeconomic and occupational profile of Soviet Jewry did not change. Jews may not have become productive through agrarianization, but plenty of opportunities existed for Jews to hold jobs in the new urban and industrial economy that emerged beginning in the 1930s. The destruction of private enterprise and trade from the late 1920s onward meant that Soviet Jews had to find new sources of income. They did so by taking advantage of opportunities provided by industrialization, urbanization, and the spread of the educational system to refashion themselves as white-collar and professional workers (engineers, teachers, doctors, managers, bookkeepers, and clerks) whose technical skills were needed by a country struggling to modernize. This trend continued throughout the era of communism: on the eve of the collapse of the Soviet Union in 1991, the vast majority of employed Jews were concentrated in non-manual occupations. Still, many Soviet Jews also found work as manual workers in the booming industrial sector or transferred their skills as artisans to state-owned and state-operated factories. No longer able to "exploit" non-Jews through their purported control of the economy, Jews in the Soviet Union, like everyone else, became employees of the state, which exploited all members of society in equal measure. Soviet Jews become integral members of the socialist economy and society. As with the religious and cultural questions, the basis of the socioeconomic question, which occupied the minds of tsarist and communist policymakers since the late eighteenth century, grew weaker as a result of government policies and the transformation of society and economy.

CHAPTER 4
THE POLITICAL QUESTION: SUBVERSION AND DISLOYALTY

A broad cross-section of tsarist society believed that Jews posed a threat to the political integrity, stability, and security of the empire and its people. This belief dovetailed with the idea prevalent throughout Europe that Jews comprised a subversive element that destabilized society through a combination of political ideas and organizations. Following in the footsteps of political conservatives throughout Europe, supporters of tsarism associated Jews with political radicalism and attributed opposition to the autocracy to the machinations of Jews. Jews purportedly lacked the commitment expected of patriotic Russians to the well-being of the state and society. Defenders of the status quo believed that Jews were an existential menace to Russia, which needed to defend itself from the onslaught engineered by Jewish opposition forces, nationalist and revolutionary alike. The loyalty of Jews to the tsarist state, be it autocratic or communist, was dubious given that Jews, it was believed, felt stronger ties to Jews in other countries. During the nineteenth and early twentieth centuries tsarist officials and intellectuals seeking to bolster the autocracy viewed Jews as intent on weakening tsarist rule through separatist ambitions or revolution. Drawing on many of the same beliefs, the communist regime after 1917 continued to accuse Soviet Jews of political disloyalty.

In the late nineteenth century the tsarist government faced challenges brought about by the proliferation of organizations that sought to reform, if not destroy, the autocracy. Many educated Russians embraced liberal and revolutionary ideas that they hoped would be the foundation of a new country dedicated to civil liberties, political freedom, and the amelioration of the appalling living and working conditions of most people, primarily peasants. Like many other educated and disaffected people living in tsarist Russia who wanted to bring progressive change to the empire, young Jewish men and women (women comprised nearly one quarter of Jews involved in the revolutionary movement in the 1870s) embraced efforts to spark peasant insurrection in the 1870s, played key roles in various revolutionary organizations determined to bring the autocratic regime to its knees, and abetted the assassination of Tsar Alexander II in 1881. The emergence of revolutionary socialist organizations during the second half of the nineteenth century deepened the conviction among officials and educated Russians that Jews were a politically subversive element intent on overthrowing the tsarist regime. Supporters of the autocracy viewed Jews as disloyal subjects of the tsar who were responsible for the troubles besetting the country by the end of the century. The disproportionate number of Jews arrested for their participation in these groups "confirmed the longstanding conviction of tsarist officials that the Jews were a particularly hardy and volatile element accounting for much of the political unrest of the two decades between 1870 and 1890."[1]

Concern about the subversive nature of Jews was confirmed by the participation of a Jewish woman, Gesia Gelfman, in the murder of Tsar Alexander II. Like other Jewish men and women who embraced revolution, Gelfman's journey to radical politics involved both repudiation of Judaism and traditional Jewish life and a conscious decision to help peasants and workers to free themselves of social and economic exploitation. For Jewish women, in particular, it required them to reject expectations that they would fulfill traditional gender roles such as marrying and raising a family. In Gelfman's case, she left home at sixteen in order to avoid an arranged marriage with a Talmudic scholar. She gravitated to radical circles because they offered a welcoming home for a young Jewish woman who wanted to dedicate her life to creating a just and egalitarian society. As one revolutionary comrade noted, Gelfman was "the embodiment of everything lofty, excellent, altruistic, and ideal. She was self-sacrificing in matters large and small." Another radical activist wrote that Gelfman "was a very sensitive person and her life was one of continuous sacrifice;

she had the ability to love."[2] Condemned to death, Gelfman was spared execution by the tsar who postponed the carrying out of the sentence because she was pregnant. A public campaign convinced the tsar to commute her death sentence to one of imprisonment, but Gelfman died of complications after giving birth to a baby who was subsequently sent to an orphanage.

Beginning in the 1880s radical Jewish youths began to embrace Marxism, which was taking root in the Russian Empire.[3] They played prominent roles in the articulation and dissemination of the revolutionary ideas of Karl Marx and Friedrich Engels and dedicated their lives to spreading the gospel of Marxism among factory and workshop employees. Marxist political parties remained predominantly non-Jewish in membership and leadership, but the percentage of Jews in such organizations exceeded the proportion of Jews in the population at large.

Jewish workers were concentrated in small workshops rather than factories, but the fact that they were not members of the industrial proletariat who would usher in the age of socialism did not mean that Jewish Marxist activists shied away from propagandizing and organizing the hundreds of thousands of Jews, both men and women, who endured harsh working conditions in small manufacturing workshops. Nor did it mean that Jewish workers shied away from the appeals of Marxist revolutionaries. In 1897 Jewish Marxists formed the Bund (formally the General Jewish Workers' Union in Lithuania, Poland, and Russia), which was committed to the transformation of tsarist Russia into a socialist society through proletarian revolution based on the principles of Marx and Engels. Bundists believed that they and not the mainstream Marxist organization (known as the Russian Social Democratic Labor Party) should exercise full control of efforts to organize Jewish workers. Bundists argued that only like-minded revolutionaries who spoke Yiddish could effectively mobilize Jewish workers not conversant in Russian and coordinate efforts to bring revolution to the country. The Bund focused on organizing Jewish workers in workshops and factories, and its membership (somewhere in the neighborhood of 30,000) far outstripped that of other Marxist political parties by the early years of the twentieth century.

In October 1905 a broad cross-section of society came close to toppling the autocracy during Russia's first brush with revolution in the twentieth century.[4] The empire was beginning to fray at its edges as various national minorities bristled at those measures of the government that suppressed their languages and cultures and promoted the centrality of the Russian language and culture. Moreover, middle-of-the road political organizations and radical groups had been advancing platforms aimed at diluting, if not eliminating, the autocracy. Beginning in late 1904, liberal, socialist, and labor organizations demanded political reforms, and various national minorities such as Poles and Finns also organized to wrest autonomy from the tsarist regime. After ten months of social and political unrest, including a general strike that brought life to a standstill, Nicholas II's empire was teetering. It was only a bold move by the tsar, at the urging of his main advisor Sergei Witte, that saved the autocracy by giving it a breathing spell that would allow it to regroup and reassert tsarist authority. In mid-October Nicholas II announced the granting civil and political rights (such as freedom of speech, press, and assembly) and establishment of a popularly elected legislative assembly. The tsar's concessions, known as the October Manifesto, legalized political parties and organizations representing a gamut of political positions: from staunch defenders of the autocracy to liberals (which included many Jewish professionals such as lawyers and academics) seeking the promulgation of a constitutional monarchy and revolutionaries intent on overthrowing the entire social and political order. The regime's reforms enabled it to weather the crisis, splitting the opposition between those willing to countenance the concessions granted by the tsar and those who viewed the reforms as inadequate. While Jews figured among those who demanded the dilution of autocratic power, they did not play a leading role in the opposition, which included liberals and revolutionaries of all stripes. Nonetheless, defenders of autocracy wasted no time in blaming Jews for the assault on the regime.

The drawing shown in Figure 4.1 appeared in a 1907 issue of *Veche* (The Realm), a staunch, pro-government newspaper that maintained that Jews were responsible for the trouble besetting the

Figure 4.1 *The New Kike Garden*

Veche (The Realm), no. 92 (November 26, 1906). Courtesy of The Bridge Research Network

autocracy. The drawing underscores the belief among supporters of tsarism that Jews threatened the political order. Captioned "The New Kike Garden," the drawing depicts a Jewish man holding a watering can who is cultivating the next generation of radical Jewish youth dressed in student uniforms and holding daggers and guns. The writing on the watering can refers to the liberal organization (Union for the Attainment of Full Civil Rights for Jews in Russia) dedicated to the attainment of civil liberties and political rights for Jews that emerged in the aftermath of Russia's first experience with revolution.

Similar messages appeared in other issues of *Veche*. In Figure 4.2 a bat with the head of a Jewish man and wings emblazoned with the word "anarchy" is about to alight on a sleeping woman identified as "Mother Russia" in order to suck her blood. In keeping with the Dracula story, the approach is implicitly sexual, an image that drew on antisemitic notions about hypersexualized male Jews preying on innocent Russian women.[5] The caption reads, "A Fitful Sleep, but Waking Up Will Be Sweet" because a *bogatyr* (a medieval Russian knight) holding a sword with the words "Union of Russian People" written on its blade is in the process of smiting the Jew-bat. The Union of Russian People, popularly known as the Black Hundreds, was one of several right-wing political organizations that emerged during the revolutionary unrest of 1905: It was unabashedly antisemitic and nationalistic, and it affixed all blame for the autocracy's problems on Jews who allegedly embraced subversive ideologies such as liberalism, anarchism, and socialism.

Figure 4.3, which appeared in an issue of the journal *Pliuvium*, highlights the insistence by defenders of the government that Jews sought to dominate the country by exploiting the civil and political liberties such as freedom of speech, press, and assembly granted in October 1905. The drawing shows a Jewish man (albeit without beard and sidelocks and traditional garb) kneeling on the lid of a coffin as he tries to hammer it shut on Mother Russia, who is struggling to prevent herself from being buried alive. Yet again the drawing underscores the victimization of Russian women by Jewish men. The coffin lid is labeled "constitution," and the wooden mallet has the words "Kike press" written on one side. These phrases underscore the claim that Jews were taking advantage of utilizing the freedom of the press and other newly granted civil liberties to bury Russia with a constitution. Even though the tsar's October Manifesto fell

Figure 4.2 A Fitful Sleep, but Waking Up Will Be Sweet

Veche (The Realm), no. 11 (January 28, 1907). Courtesy of The Bridge Research Network

short of creating a genuine constitutional monarchy, the right-wing press seized on the word 'constitution' to refer to the newly acquired political freedoms in the fall of 1905 that they believed represented an existential threat to Russia and threatened the foundation of the autocracy.

Вколачиваніе въ гробъ заживо.

Figure 4.3 Buried Alive

Pliuvium, no. 43 (July 28, 1907), 2. Courtesy of The Bridge Research Network

Pogroms were another expression of the rejection of political modernity by supporters of the monarchy. Derived from the Russian verb *gromit'*, which means to smash, destroy, or shatter, the word "pogrom" has come to mean violent attacks on Jews and their property. The word first emerged to describe riots that targeted Jews in the aftermath of the assassination of Tsar Alexander II in 1881.[6] Dozens of pogroms occurred in 1881 and 1882 after a group of revolutionaries blew up Tsar Alexander II with a bomb. Defenders of the autocracy were quick to blame Jews, but economic resentment and unemployment also played a role in stimulating the anti-Jewish popular unrest that punctured the social stability of the major cities of Odesa, Kyiv, and Warsaw as well as small towns and shtetls in primarily the southern region of the Pale of Settlement. The pogrom in Kishinev, Moldova, in the spring of 1903 was another key development in popular violence against Jews. Not only did the violence stun the public inside and outside the empire, but the attack on Kishinev's Jews gave rise to the phenomenon of Jewish self-defense brigades that henceforth materialized whenever outbursts of antisemitic unrest threaten Jewish lives and property. By the turn of the twentieth century, pogrom had entered English, Russian, and other languages to refer to the waves of anti-Jewish violence that occurred during the final decades of tsarist rule. Pogroms took place in the context of political crisis and widespread social unrest and revealed the dark underbelly of Russian society and politics.

The outburst of anti-Jewish violence occurred in 1905 at the height of the revolutionary unrest. The pogroms of 1905 were considerably more violent, deadly, and destructive than those a quarter century earlier. But they did not reach the levels of bloodshed experienced in 1918–21, when the collapse of state authority and fighting among contending armies during the civil war that broke out after the seizure of power by the Bolsheviks in 1917 resulted in the largest loss of Jewish life prior to the Second World War. In terms of death and destruction, the pogroms of 1905 were a way station between those of 1881–2 and 1918–21, when marauding soldiers engaged in wanton, unrestrained violence against Jews. In 1881–2 rioters primarily targeted property and shouted "Beat the Yids," but deaths numbered no more than a few dozen. In 1905, however, pogroms turned deadlier as pogromists, who were often unskilled and unemployed workers, threatened to kill, butcher, and slaughter Jews. In 1905 hundreds of Jews died at the hands of pogromists and thousands suffered injuries.

In 1905 many pogromists were motivated by a desire to punish Jews for their alleged political disloyalty, but not all the people who trashed

Figure 4.4 A pro-government procession in Odessa, October 1905

Illustrated London News (December 2, 1905), 800–1

Jewish homes, looted Jewish stores, and harmed Jews physically were acting out of political motivations. Some simply got caught up in the heat of the moment and participated in the looting and destruction of property to enrich themselves. Others blamed Jews for unemployment and other economic ills. Yet anti-Jewish violence was part of the arsenal of conservative forces who rejected the efforts to bring liberal political reform to autocratic Russia. In 1905, for example, speakers at meetings hosted by antisemitic organizations denounced socialism as the bedfellow of political subversion. In an early version of "Russian Lives Matter" or "Russia First," Russian nationalists demanded that Russians be masters in their country.

The association of Jews with radical political movements remained a constant feature of antisemitic forces after 1917. Domestic opponents of communism, particularly during the civil war that ravaged the country between 1918 and 1921, relied in part on antisemitism to mobilize armies and motivate soldiers. Often at the instigation of their commanders, soldiers fighting for the anti-Bolshevik White forces or an independent Ukraine set upon Jewish men, women, and children, motivated by the popular identification of "Bolshevism as a quintessentially Jewish doctrine."[7] Their commanders shared this view, which became known as the "myth of Judeo-Bolshevism," a canard fundamental to Nazi ideology. The pogroms that gripped the country after the war graduated to ethnic cleansing and, in the minds of some scholars, genocide. Estimates vary but at least 100,000 Jews died at the hands of peasants, townspeople, and soldiers on both sides of the conflict, and the destruction of Jewish houses and businesses worsened the poverty and displacement of Jews. Hundreds of thousands of Jews were wounded or died from injuries received during pogroms as well as disease. Moreover, tens of thousands of Jewish women of all ages were raped by marauding soldiers who acted with impunity.[8]

The Jews' purported desire to subvert the autocracy through revolution was paralleled by the accusation of separatist ambitions. This concern can be traced back to the early decades of the nineteenth century when tsarist ministers blamed the kahal, the communal institution that oversaw the affairs of the Jewish community, for Russian Jewry's failure to integrate. Under tsarist rule, Jews—like other religious minorities—enjoyed a degree of self-government and autonomy when it came to the internal affairs of the community. As the executive body that ruled the Jewish community and represented it to state authorities, the kahal exercised judicial, administrative, and economic control. It managed Jewish affairs, determining who would be conscripted into the military, who would collect taxes, and who was in charge of policing and administering justice. This state of affairs led many officials to contend that the institutionalized autonomy of the Jewish community prevented the rapprochement of Jewish and non-Jewish society and stymied efforts at Jewish integration.

A law of 1844 abolished the kahal, which meant that the state now exercised greater supervision of the Jewish community. But the law did not end the right of Jews in tsarist Russia to control religious affairs and other matters related to Jewish life. Despite this effort to legislate out of existence the institutional expression of Jewish autonomy and self-governance, suspicions remained that the kahal was still operating in violation of the law and hindering government control. Iakov Brafman, a convert to Russian Orthodoxy, led the campaign to challenge the kahal's authority. In *The Book of the Kahal*, which first appeared in the late 1860s, Brafman claimed to have uncovered documents from the Jewish community of Minsk that demonstrated communal institutions, not the Talmud and other Judaic texts, accounted for Russian Jewry's supposed religious fanaticism and stubborn aversion to changes in their way of life.[9] According to Brafman, the kahal subordinated the life of individual Jews to the authority of the community's social and economic elite, which maintained control by imposing educational, cultural, religious, and economic regulations. The unrestrained power of the kahal enabled the Jewish community's leadership to impose disciplinary measures on troublemakers and others who challenged the rule of the kahal, especially if they wanted to engage in behavior that weakened communal solidarity and traditional religious values. Brafman also asserted that individual kahals comprised larger entities that transcended local communities and acquired national and even international importance. In his view, Jewish communal institutions endeavored to spread Jewish influence throughout the world. As Brafman wrote, kahals united on an international level in order "to prepare in Judaism everything necessary to attain its highest goals, the resurrection of an independent Jewish entity," that is, a Jewish state.[10]

The Book of the Kahal served as one inspiration for *The Protocols of the Elders of Zion*, a fabricated and much publicized account published in Russia at the start of the twentieth century about the purported global effort of Jews to control the world. The *Protocols* claimed to be the record of secret meetings of Jewish religious and secular leaders conspiring to promote Jewish domination of the world. Written and published by Pavel Krushevan, a notorious antisemitic writer and newspaper publisher who helped trigger the 1903 pogrom in Kishinev, Moldova, the book highlights the alleged threat posed by a cabal of Jews to Russia and the rest of the world.[11] By the 1920s the *Protocols* had become the most widely distributed antisemitic publication throughout Europe and the United States, had been translated into multiple languages, and provided antisemites with the language and arguments, no matter how faulty, to condemn Jews wherever they lived. To this day the forgery remains a chief weapon in the arsenal of antisemites, neo-Nazis, and white nationalists.

Krushevan's novel *What Is Russia?*, written in the mid-1890s, presaged the views expressed in the *Protocols*. According to the protagonist of the book, the Jews' desire for global domination posed an existential threat to Russia. Russia's Jews hindered efforts to resolve the Jewish question because they refused to assimilate into Russian society and culture and maintained their isolation from Christian society. The novel's protagonist concluded that it should come as no surprise that the Jews' economic exploitation of non-Jews triggered violence.[12]

The *Protocols* is a diatribe about the concerted efforts of an international Jewish conspiracy to use whatever mean available to assert Jewish power and amass wealth. To the author (or authors) of the *Protocols*, Jews were the malicious forces behind the social and political movements of modernity such as liberalism, socialism of all stripes, democracy, anarchism, and finance capitalism that sought to exploit and control non-Jews. Protocol Number 1 asserts,

> Our motto is Power and Hypocrisy. Only power can conquer in politics, especially if it is concealed in talents which are necessary to statesmen.... we must not hesitate at bribery, fraud and treason when these can help us to reach our end. In politics it is necessary to seize the property of others without hesitation if in so doing we attain submission and power.[13]

The *Protocols* claim to expose the underlying motivations of Jews to use whatever means possible to take advantage of non-Jews. Many aspects of the Jewish question as it emerged and developed in tsarist Russia and the Soviet Union found resonance in the *Protocols*, which has been a mainstay of antisemitic thought from its appearance until today.

The consolidation of Bolshevik power after 1917 brought about a reversal of some aspects of government policy regarding Jews.[14] The perceived association of Jews with socialism was no longer condemned but something to be fostered and celebrated. The strong stance that Vladimir Lenin, leader of the Bolshevik regime, took against antisemitism, along with the party's effort to stamp out all expressions of anti-Jewish prejudice, discrimination, and violence, encouraged Jews to embrace the fledgling communist government, which guaranteed full civil and political rights for Jews. But the communist government was not entirely free of antisemitism. At the same time many in the leadership were dedicated to ending anti-Jewish prejudices and behavior, some high-ranking Bolsheviks were indifferent to the problem. Moreover, many rank-and-file party members, along with many workers, held antisemitic views such as the association they made about the supposed outsized role that Jews played in the continued existence of capitalist values and practices during the transition to socialism. The party's leadership had to combat antisemitism not only among many workers but also among rank-and-file party members: "the notion that Bolshevism could appeal to far-right antisemites was not without substance …. Revolutionary politics and antisemitism could go hand in hand."[15]

For anti-Bolsheviks, however, the fact that some prominent Bolsheviks such as Leon Trotsky, Grigorii Zinoviev, and Lev Kamenev came from Jewish families and that many Jews staffed the Cheka (the All-Russian Extraordinary Commission for Combating Counter-Revolution and Sabotage, the first incarnation of the Soviet Union's secret police) confirmed the belief that Jews were responsible for the world's first government committed to the building of socialism.[16] A "special relationship" existed between Bolsheviks and Jews," an apt appraisal of the role Jews played in the communist movement elsewhere in Europe, the United States, Canada, and South America.[17] The young regime's promise to promote Jewish equality and freedom and the disproportionate share of Jews in high-ranking positions in the Communist Party and government institutions confirmed the belief of the regime's opponents that Jews were responsible for the troubles besetting Russia even before 1917. The Communist Party was aware that the perception that Jews were overrepresented in leadership roles and other positions of responsibility fueled popular antisemitism and detracted from the appeal of communism. Indeed, by the 1930s the

Kremlin went out of its way to mask the participation of Jews in party and government institutions so as not to fan the flames of grassroots antisemitism. In addition, in 1939 Stalin replaced Maxim Litvinov, a Jew, as minister of foreign affairs with the non-Jew Vyacheslav Molotov in order to curry favor with Hitler.

Figure 4.5, drawn in 1919 by an anticommunist artist in Poland and entitled *Peace and Freedom in the Land of the Soviet Deputies*, underscores this perceived linkage between Bolshevism and Jews. The man sitting on the walls of the Kremlin is Leon Trotsky, who was the number two man, after Lenin, in the Bolshevik Party. It was well-known that Trotsky was of Jewish background (his given name was Lev Bronshtein), and in this caricature he sports a gold Star of David and resembles an outsized monster who has red skin and inhuman hands and feet that have dripped blood onto the walls. He looks over a pile of skulls, presumably killed by the soldiers standing on them. This depiction of the blood-thirsty nature of Bolshevik power with the Jew Trotsky in command reinforces the myth of Judeo-Bolshevism. The fact that the soldiers have non-Slavic facial characteristics drives home the point that the communist regime drew sustenance from the participation of people deemed less civilized and more savage than Russians and Europeans.

As in tsarist times, the political loyalty of Jews loomed large for supporters of communism and was never far from the minds of government policymakers. The worry that Jews harbored a "dual loyalty" to the country in which they lived and to worldwide Jewry was a persistent concern for the communist government. Officials viewed national sentiments among Jews (not to mention other national minorities, especially those living along the border of the country) as a threat to the international solidarity of workers, labeling such attitudes as manifestations of "bourgeois nationalism." After all, Jews proclaimed at the end of the Passover Seder "Next year in Jerusalem," all the more reason to suppress religious observance and political activity among Jews.

The communist regime's concern about Jewish separatism and nationalism remained a key element of the Kremlin's policy, an outlook reminiscent of pre-1917 tsarism's fears of Jews' disloyalty and

Figure 4.5 *Peace and Freedom in the Land of the Soviet Deputies* (1919)

Courtesy of Manuscript and Archives Division, The New York Public Library, Astor, Lenox and Tilden Foundations

lack of allegiance. The government hounded the Bund out of existence because it was seen as a divisive force that elevated Jewish concerns above those serving the interests of all workers, regardless of ethnicity or nationality. Along similar lines, the Kremlin outlawed Zionism, the political movement that demanded the restoration of an independent Jewish state in the Land of Israel. Policymakers worried that if Soviet Jewry embraced the Zionist cause, it would be yet another indication that Jews saw themselves as a "state within a state" and did not view the Soviet Union as their homeland. By the end of the 1920s the regime suppressed any expression of Zionist activity: the government arrested, imprisoned, and exiled thousands of Jews active in Zionist organizations. The lucky ones were expelled from the country, only to find refuge in Palestine, Europe, and the United States. Those who escaped the vigilant eye of the state continued their illegal activities by going underground where they studied Hebrew and read Hebrew literature, which had also been suppressed as a manifestation of Jewish nationalism and religion. Intensification of the regime's harsh persecution of independent Jewish life during the 1930s made it all but impossible for Zionists to continue their activities. By the mid-1930s manifestations of Zionist thought and organization had been extinguished.

A convincing case can be made that government policies paradoxically reinforced self-identification as Jews. When the Kremlin issued internal passports in the early 1930s, the identification of Jews by their nationality—Jewish—made it well-nigh impossible for Soviet Jews to escape official recognition as Jews. This designation on a document that all Soviet citizens carried on their person and presented in all official circumstances made it easy to identify Jews and subject them to discriminatory practices. It also reinforced Soviet Jews' sense of Jewish identity, notwithstanding the fact that they had begun to integrate and acculturate into non-Jewish society and culture, a trend that continued until the collapse of the Soviet Union.

In the aftermath of the Second World War concern about Soviet Jewry's loyalty as citizens acquired even greater significance.[18] The outbreak of the Cold War heightened tensions between the West and Soviet Union, and the decision by the Kremlin to promote

Russocentric policies, which had begun in the 1930s, that limited Jewish representation in cultural and academic endeavors, along with the establishment of the independent state of Israel in 1948, contributed to an official campaign to malign Soviet Jews as bourgeois nationalists. The enthusiastic welcome of Golda Meir, Israel's first ambassador to the Soviet Union, when she visited the Moscow Choral Synagogue during Rosh Hashanah services in 1948, unnerved the Kremlin. The fact that thousands of Soviet Jews cheered Meir and voiced their support for the independent Jewish state reinforced the government's suspicion that Jews had divided political loyalties and posed a threat to the communist regime.

During the five years preceding Stalin's death in early 1953, the Kremlin engaged in a systematic campaign that targeted Jewish cultural institutions and personages: the state closed Yiddish publishing houses and theaters and, in 1948, Solomon Mikhoels, the best-known Jewish actor in the Soviet Union, was run over by a truck in an accident staged by the government. The authorities' responsibility for Mikhoels's death did not stop the government from cynically giving him a funeral fitting for a cultural luminary.

Soon after Mikhoels's death, the government arrested a group of prominent Jews. In August 1952 a secret trial found fourteen Jewish academics, writers, actors, and scientists guilty of treason and espionage on trumped-up evidence in August of that year, which has become known as "The Night of the Murdered Poets" because several defendants were the crème de la crème poets who wrote in Yiddish. Thirteen of the fourteen defendants were executed; one of the two women on trial was spared the death sentence.[19] Many had been active in the Jewish Anti-Fascist Committee, an organization established by the Kremlin to rally support by the American Jewish community for the war effort against Nazi Germany. Those executed enjoyed state support for their work in the 1920s and survived the purges of the 1930s, only to find themselves victims of government policies that found any expression of Jewish culture, such as writing in Yiddish, a sign of anti-Soviet attitudes and bourgeois nationalism. For example, some members of the Jewish Anti-Fascist Committee were condemned for floating the idea of establishing a full-fledged Jewish republic on the

Crimean Peninsula that would supplant Birobidzhan as the putative homeland of Soviet Jews and be the first step in dismantling the Soviet Union. Others were condemned for living abroad in the 1920s and 1930s and supposedly revealing government secrets to foreigners.[20] It was not until the liberalization of political life under Mikhail Gorbachev during the second half of the 1980s that the government admitted that the trials and executions were a gross miscarriage of justice.

The Kremlin also labeled Soviet Jews as "rootless cosmopolitans" who did not consider the Soviet Union their homeland. The regime initiated a concerted campaign that viciously questioned their patriotism and loyalty, an attack that culminated in early 1953 in what has become known as the Doctors' Plot. The government arrested several dozen doctors and their spouses, many of whom were Jewish, and accused them of conspiring to murder government and party officials. The Kremlin posited the alleged affinity between the capitalist West and the arrested "doctor-saboteurs" who were condemned for working hand in hand with the enemies of the Soviet Union, namely the United States, Great Britain, and Zionists, and engaging in terrorist actions that threatened the security of the Soviet Union. The Kremlin insisted that "all members of the terrorist group of physicians were hired agents of foreign intelligence services. The heinous crimes of these monsters, who had lost every human semblance, were controlled by the American and British intelligence services" and were supported by an "international Jewish bourgeois-nationalist organization" engaging in "sordid Zionist espionage."[21]

The persecution of the Jewish doctors sparked an outburst of officially sanctioned anti-Jewish animus that highlighted the persistence of the Jewish question. To be sure, the portrayal of Jews in the press relied on timeworn antisemitic images and prejudices. But the impetus for the anti-Jewish campaign had less to do with antisemitic hatred and more to do with the regime's perception that the behavior of Soviet Jews breached the boundaries of acceptable expressions of the country's nationality policy. For example, Figure 4.6 depicts how the hand of the Soviet Union has unmasked an enemy, who had disguised himself as a doctor and was in the paid employ of the capitalist West. The Doctors' Plot revealed the regime's conviction that Soviet Jews

Figure 4.6 Evidence of a Crime

Krokodil (Crocodile) (January 1953). Courtesy of The Bridge Research Network

attempted to hide who they really are, namely masked traitors. They may have behaved as if they want to integrate into Soviet society but digging below the surface revealed that they never can. Blood on the fingertips of the Jewish doctor was a not very subtle allusion to the blood libel. The emergence of open government hostility toward Jews in the 1940s led to a revival of the blood libel. Newspapers and radio echoed the Kremlin's vitriol, and the public response drew upon the time-worn blood libel, which had persisted under communist rule. Moreover, the accusation became detached from religion as Jews were targeted for killing non-Jews for political purposes rather than the fulfillment of religious commands.

The public campaign against Jewish doctors in early 1953 sparked extreme reactions among Russians. Rumors abounded: Jewish doctors were accused of poisoning and murdering Russian children and infecting them with deadly diseases such as cancer; apartment dwellers worried that their Jewish neighbors were intent on poisoning their food in the communal kitchens they shared; and Jews were set upon by angry Russians who spat and shouted epithets at them in public. One Soviet Jew documented the abuse and fear she and others faced at the height of the Doctor's Plot. She wrote that the "Christian women who share kitchen facilities with Jews have begun to make the lives of the latter miserable; Christian children direct vulgar, insolent remarks at Jewish adults."[22] A Jewish tractor driver on a collective farm in Ukraine noted that during "the Doctors' Plot, people began to point at us, saying, `Jews, Jews, Jews.' Whenever I went to a store, or to a street, I would hear, `A Yid, a Yid, you poisoned people."[23] In general, Soviet Jews were on edge and feared the worst as they anticipated physical violence, persecution, loss of work, imprisonment, and life in Siberian exile.

Not all non-Jews abused Jews, however. One Jewish man recollected how a neighbor in his building came to his defense when news of the Doctor's Plot was reported in the press: "Janitors gathered outside the entrance to our housing complex. A neighbour of mine who lived in the same building stood in the middle. When she saw me, she started waving a newspaper and said to the janitors in a loud voice so that I could hear her: 'He is a good man. They are all good people.'"[24] The death of Stalin in early March 1953 marked the end of the matter as his successors released the physicians from prison and dropped charges against them. The public outcry against Soviet Jews, which bordered on mass hysteria, dissipated because government support for it had been withdrawn. Jews could breathe more easily and no longer fear that they would lose their jobs or face open condemnation.

The political loyalty of Soviet Jews remained in question even after Stalin's death. State-sponsored anti-Jewish propaganda associated synagogues with illegal economic dealings, anti-Soviet agitation, and Zionist activism. The Jews' alleged allegiance to Israel trumped their fealty to the Soviet Union and placed them under a pall of constant suspicion, reinforcing popular prejudices that Jews felt greater attachment to world Jewry than to the Soviet Union.

***

A persistent element of the Jewish question in tsarist Russia and the Soviet Union was the belief that Jews were politically unreliable, engaged in an international conspiracy against Russia and loyal to Jews all over the globe. For the most part the overwhelming majority of Jews did not challenge the tsarist regime. They tended to be patriotic and did not hesitate to take up arms in defense of the state during the First World War. But there is no denying that Jews welcomed the overthrow of tsarism in 1917 that promised to usher in an age of freedom. Furthermore, some 1.5 million Jews signaled their dissatisfaction by emigrating in the decades between 1880 and 1914 in search of better lives for themselves and their families and in response to policies that fostered antisemitism and interfered with their ability to live free of state interference and discrimination. The communist regime alienated many Jews by persecuting those who were frustrated by the state's concerted antireligious policies. But the Kremlin prohibited Jewish emigration from the late 1920s to the early 1970s, when the government loosened restrictions as part of a diplomatic overture to reduce the tensions of the Cold War.

From the 1960s to the mid-1980s the Soviet government continued to enact anti-Jewish policies: numerical quotas limited, if not prohibited, Jews from enrolling in prestigious university programs such as ones that prepared students for careers in the diplomatic corps and overseas work. In the 1970s the number of Jews admitted to institutions of higher education declined by 40 percent.[25] The regime also stressed the alleged political disloyalty of Soviet Jews by highlighting their purported affinity to Jews living in Israel and the West. The fact that 240,000 Jews emigrated to Israel, Western Europe, and North America, particularly the United States, from the late 1960s to the end of the 1980s reinforced the official and popular views that Jews "could not be trusted to be loyal citizens" and led to the decision to impose onerous fees for permission to emigrate.[26] In addition, officials denied exit visas to many applicants, a trend that worsened after heightened diplomatic tensions emerged at the turn of the 1980s. Soviet Jews who had been refused exit visas were labeled "refuseniks": they had to wait until Gorbachev reversed policy in the mid-1980s and reopened the doors to emigration. The act of applying to leave the Soviet Union led to the loss of work and subjected applicants to various forms of harassment and mistreatment by officials. Not surprisingly, the Kremlin's policies, designed to discourage emigration, prompted many Soviet Jews to seek new lives in countries that welcomed them. The desire to escape antisemitism, the wish to practice Judaism freely, and the hope that their children would have better lives prompted Jews to leave the Soviet Union. Even though Soviet Jews had assimilated and integrated, their loyalty and patriotism remained in question.

EPILOGUE

By the time of Stalin's death in 1953 the Jewish question had commanded the attention of tsarist and communist policymakers for over 150 year and had remained remarkably consistent in terms of its focus and content. The Jewish question, as I have argued in this book, encompassed four sub-questions that addressed the religious, cultural, socioeconomic, and political nature of Jewish society as perceived by non-Jews (primarily Russian) living in tsarist Russia and the Soviet Union. While each question was concerned with discrete issues, the four questions blended together, addressing what Russians believed to be the problematic nature of Jewish society and culture. In particular, what explained the Jews' perceived problematic behaviors and what were the conditions by which Jews could integrate into Russian society?

During the decades between Stalin's death and 1991, when the Soviet Union collapsed, the Jewish question remained alive. It continued to preoccupy some non-Jewish observers of contemporary society and politics, notwithstanding the fact that Soviet Jews had become assimilated and integrated into non-Jewish society. The features of Jewish society that had given rise to the question in the first place no longer existed: Jews no longer spoke and dressed distinctively; most Jews no longer observed Judaism; Jews were no longer labeled the harbingers of political and economic modernity; Jews no longer stood outside the mainstream of society. In short, they had become full-fledged members of Soviet society and the basis of the Jewish question from the perspective of non-Jews had vanished. The timeworn complaints about Jews as an alien, dangerous minority found little, if no correspondence in reality.

Since the break-up of the Soviet Union in 1991 the Jewish question has occupied less of a role in politics. Government officials now pay less attention to the issue than they did under tsarism and communism. Several factors account for the diminished nature of the Jewish question and the smaller role it plays in the minds of intellectuals and politicians. First, the governments of the newly independent Russian Federation and Ukraine, where most former Soviet Jews live, aspired to be liberal polities in the 1990s, eliminating the disabilities and hindrances faced by Soviet Jews. In the 1990s President Boris Yeltsin did not sanction expressions of state-sponsored antisemitism. By the same token, however, he did not take active measures to keep in check the proliferation of anti-Jewish publications and pronouncements by right-wing Russian nationalists. Despite the illiberal trends that have characterized politics in the former Soviet Union since 2000, Vladimir Putin has shown himself to be a friend of the Jews and Israel, and has not allowed the Russian state to backslide into anti-Jewish policies. The Russian government under his rule has been much more pro-active in combating antisemitism. In addition, the election of Volodomyr Zelensky, a Jewish comedian, as president of Ukraine (which became an independent state in 1991) underscores the ability of Jews to become fully integrated into mainstream society.[1]

The decline of the Jewish question was also due to the fact that the number of Jews living in the post-Soviet world is much smaller than it was under communist rule. Between 1989 and 2019 some 1.7 million Jews left the former Soviet Union for Israel, Germany, and the United States, which brought the total number of Jews who emigrated to 2 million since 1970, when nearly 2.2 million Jews lived in the Soviet Union. By 2019 the number of Jews residing in the former Soviet Union was 248,000.[2] Of course, there is no quantitative threshold for the existence of antisemitism and the Jewish question: Jews do not need to be present for non-Jews to harbor anti-Jewish attitudes and prejudices and spout venomous ideas about the supposed threat posed by Jews. But changing demographics have led to a weakening of antisemitism and the Jewish question in contemporary Russian society. Negative views and attitudes about Jews have diminished as Russian society has become more urbanized, educated, and middle class, a trend that will continue as the older generation of Russians who lived under communist rule die.[3]

Nevertheless, the Jewish question remained alive for many Jews in the former USSR. My aunt emigrated from a suburb of St. Petersburg in 2001 out of fear of open displays of antisemitism. She was feeling the tensions of a revival of blaming Jews for the problems faced by Russia, such as economic insecurity, political instability, and loss of national prestige. Accordingly, she worried that her neighbors would break into her apartment and kill her while screaming antisemitic epithets and blaming her and other Jews for their problems. Extreme right-wing nationalists, who had begun to mobilize in the 1980s during the era of *glasnost'* under Mikhail Gorbachev, maintained a public presence during the years of Boris Yeltsin's rule in the 1990s. The best-known of these political parties was *Pamiat'* (Memory), the shortened name for the National Patriotic Front "*Pamiat'*," which promoted Orthodox Christian, conservative values, advocated for the restoration of the monarchy, and borrowed freely from the *Protocol of the Elders of Zion* to condemn Jews as agents of Zionism intent on destroying the Russian nation and its culture. Its motto was "God! Tsar! Nation!" By the end of the decade, however, the organization, debilitated by ideological divisions among its leaders and organizational splintering, had vanished from the political scene. It did re-appear in a newer reincarnation after the beginning of the twenty-first century, but its successor was a weakened version of the original organization.

Figure E.1, while not published by *Pamiat'*, reflects the persistence of the association of Jews with greater allegiance to Zionism and Israel than to their country of residence and demonstrates the tenacity of the Jewish question at the end of the twentieth century. It appeared on the front page of a 1991 issue of *Moskovskii traktir* (Moscow Tavern), a publication of the Russian National Liberation Movement, a virulently antisemitic organization opposed to the democratic and liberal trends of the Soviet Union in its dying days. Even though it was a marginal group with no political influence, its ideology drew sustenance from long-standing tropes and attitudes regarding Jews. At the top of the drawing we see a prototypical Russian worker sweeping away a group of Jewish men and women with rat tails and other distorted facial features that collapse the difference between men and women and for that matter the difference between rodents

Figure E.1 Front page of *Moskovskii traktir*

Moskovskii traktir (The Moscow Tavern), no. 1 (1991). Personal Collection of Author

and humans. Just below this drawing is one of a Jewish man holding a banner that reads: "Dem/Kike-ocracy." In other words, the cartoon suggests that democratization is simply the Jewish people's way to control post-communist Russia, a sentiment right in line with certain tropes of the Jewish question. The headline reads, "The fruits of *glasnost'* are visible everywhere. The Jews behave more impudently." The newspaper kept alive the myth of Judeo-Bolshevism by listing the names of nearly 200 persons it erroneously claimed were both Bolsheviks and Jews. Only a handful of the revolutionaries on the list were Jews, but the uninformed reader would have no idea of knowing it was inaccurate.

A more recent expression of how the Jewish question has remained alive appeared in 2012 at the time of the trial and conviction of Pussy Riot for "hooliganism motivated by religious hatred." Five members of Pussy Riot—a feminist, performance art group established in 2011 that opposes Vladmir Putin, criticizes the Russian Orthodox church, and promotes LGBTQ rights—were arrested for performing a song that called for the exorcism of Putin in the Cathedral of Christ the Savior, which is in walking distance of the Kremlin.

In response to what they believed was the sacrilegious violation of the sanctity of a place of worship, two Orthodox priests resurrected the blood libel and established what they believed to be a link between the disrespectful and profane behavior of Pussy Riot and the trial of Mendel Beilis a century earlier. One article, written by Archpriest Georgii Gorodentsev, was entitled "Pussy Riot and M. Beilis: Blasphemy in the Cathedral of Christ the Savior: Crime and Punishment." A priest by the name of Aleksandr Shumskii penned a second article entitled "Pussy Riot—A New Beilis Affair," which shared the same subtitle as the one by Gorodentsev.[4]

Shumskii left his readers with no doubt about the true nature of Pussy Riot's crime, condemning their punk prayer performance as both blasphemous and ritualistic. He wrote that what transpired in the Cathedral on the morning of February 21, 2012, was a "well thought out Satanic ritual." And just to be sure the reader understood the gravity of the offense given by Pussy Riot's performance, he noted that their clothing, body movements, and mixing of holy and spiritual words during the punk prayer "testifies to the ritual nature of the blasphemy."

Likewise, Gorodentsev referred to Pussy Riot as "Raging Uterus" (*Bzbesivshaiasia matka*), presumably because he felt "Pussy Riot" was too crude. He accused the five women who performed the impromptu concert of committing "a ritual crime" that aimed to enlist the Russian people in the "ritual defilement" of the cathedral. He went so far as to label what Pussy Riot did as "the action of the possessed." In addition, and perhaps for the benefit of those readers who needed help to draw the proper conclusions, the archpriest referred to a book published in 1914 by the Russian Orthodox priest, T. I. Butkevich, about the meaning and significance of blood sacrifice, with a particular emphasis on ritual murder.

Drawing upon Butkevich, Gorodentsev noted that until the beginning of the nineteenth century people accused of ritual murder were severely punished, a situation that began to change during the course of the 1800s. Since the start of the twentieth century, Gorodentsev claimed, ritual murders tended to go undiscovered, and in those instances when alleged murderers were arrested and prosecuted, chances were that the suspects were found innocent and set free. For Gorodentsev, the failure to find Beilis guilty of ritual murder turned him into the victim in the eyes of the public, while no one was held accountable for the murder of the Christian boy, Andrei Iushchinskii. Gorodentsev saw the prosecution of Pussy Riot as a "decisive victory" of the Russian people against the efforts of "progressive Russian society" to undermine the Orthodox values that undergird Russia. The conviction and incarceration of Pussy Riot would signify the first step in the battle against the existential enemies of Russia such as those involved in ritual murder as well as the carriers of depraved Western values and culture. In short, both men of the cloth stressed what they believed was the demonic nature of Pussy Riot's performance. They asserted that Pussy Riot was part of a Western conspiracy to undermine Russian Orthodoxy, the Russian people, and Russian culture. In the words of the lawyers defending the church, Pussy Riot uses "deception to lead the flock not to God, but to Satan."[5]

Similarities between the trials of Pussy Riot and Mendel Beilis abound, particularly in terms of the role of the government, the responses across the political spectrum, and public awareness and debate both at home and abroad share many common features. Indeed, both trials reflected the cultural, ideological, and political fissures that characterized Russian society under the rule of Putin and Nicholas II. For example, Russian patriots believed then, much as they do now, that Russia was under siege by the West. In the case of Beilis, Jews were responsible for efforts to undermine Russian culture and values, and in the case of Pussy Riot liberalism and secularism were the challenge. In addition, just as liberals, socialists, and other progressive thinkers condemned the autocracy at the time of the Beilis Affair, the defenders of Pussy Riot, namely the "liberal intelligentsia," are also critics of Putin and his government. At issue in both cases was the preservation of the genuine Russia. One significant difference is that Orthodox theologians tended to defend Beilis and asserted that there was no truth to the blood libel. Indeed, the prosecution during the Beilis trial could not find one Russian Orthodox theologian or priest who would testify on its behalf. A century later, however, the leadership of the Russian Orthodox Church vigorously attacked Pussy Riot, though it did not embrace the myth of the blood libel.

The ritualistic nature of the two events, at least according to Shumskii, links them in a significant manner. Pussy Riot blasphemed and desecrated a holy space by performing a song designed to be an exorcism ("Mother of God, Drive Out Putin"), and Beilis, along with several other unknown Jews, purportedly engaged in a ritual killing ordained by Judaic law. In both cases, Beilis and Pussy Riot were accused of behavior that challenged the Christian norms and values of Russian society. And the threats posed by Russia's enemies were alien to Russian culture and society: Western secular values in the case of Pussy Riot and Judaism in the case of Beilis. Curiously, Gorodentsev did not use the word "Jew," but Shumskii did refer to the "Jew Beilis." However, the words "ritual murder" and "blood libel" are associated with the words "Jew" and "Judaism" among many Russians and resonate strongly among those who believe Jews pose an existential threat to Christian culture, society, and values. It is not far-fetched to think that those church officials who condemn Pussy Riot as part of the West's effort to destroy Russia also believe that the international Jewish-Masonic conspiracy is at work in Putin's Russia today (though it is worth noting that the Russian Orthodox Church officially disowns antisemitism). Both the antisemites who insisted that Jews engage in ritual murder and the church officials who condemned Pussy Riot share the belief that Russia was under siege, a world view that was illiberal, anti-Western, and antisemitic.

***

These trends and developments indicate that the Jewish question in Russia has not run its course. No amount of government pressure or changing realities will alter how people prone to embrace conspiracy theories will think and behave. Nevertheless, the Jewish question has been relegated to the fringes of the political spectrum in Russia, though this does not mean it is absent from Russian society and politics. But the remnants of what once was the largest community of Jews in the world in the early twentieth century live, for the most part, in a country with a government and people that no longer view Jews as an existential threat.

GLOSSARY OF TERMS

Blood Libel/Ritual Murder: False accusation that Jews murder Christian youths whose blood is required for Jewish religious rituals.

Bolsheviks/Communist Party: Political party led by Vladimir Lenin that established the regime in 1917 and ruled the Soviet Union until 1991.

Haskalah **(Jewish Enlightenment):** Intellectual and social movement that encouraged the social, economic, cultural, and political integration of Jews into gentile society.

Kheyder: Elementary school where Jewish boys learned Hebrew and the fundamentals of Judaism.

Kosher: Foods that conform to laws of *kashrut*, Jewish dietary law.

Pale of Settlement: The region of the Russian Empire in which Jews were required to reside.

Partitions of Polish-Lithuanian Commonwealth: Russia, Prussia, and Austria divided up the territory of Poland and Lithuania at the end of the eighteenth century.

Pogroms: Violent, anti-Jewish riots.

Talmud: Compendium of rabbinical discussions about the Torah.

Torah: Hebrew Scriptures or the Old Testament.

Yarmulke: Skullcap worn by Jewish men.

Yeshiva: School where young Jewish men studied Talmud and the laws that govern daily Jewish life.

Glossary of Terms

Yiddish: Language of Eastern European Jews.

Zionism: Political philosophy and movement that advocated the establishment of a sovereign Jewish state.

NOTES

Introduction

1   In an alternative reading, socio-linguist Rakhmiel Peltz suggests that the sibilant "s" may not refer to a speech impediment but may reflect the sibilant sounds in the Yiddish spoken by some Jews living in the Russian Empire. Rakhmiel Peltz, "The Sibilants of Northeastern Yiddish: A Study in Linguistic Variation," in Marvin Herzog, Ulrike Kiefer, Robert Neumann, Wolfgang Putschke, and Andrew Sunshine, eds., *EYDES (Evidence of Yiddish Documented in European Societies): The Language and Culture Atlas of Ashkenazic Jewry)* (Tubingen: Max Niemeyer Verlag, 2008), 242–73.

2   Holly Case, *The Age of Questions* (Princeton: Princeton University Press, 2018).

3   The four questions refer to the queries asked at the Passover seder, the meal that recounts the Jews' exodus from Egypt to the land promised to the descendants of Abraham. In addition, I use the words "question" and "problem" interchangeably, especially since the Russian word *vopros* can be translated as either "question" or "problem." In common parlance, however, beginning in the nineteenth century, European society addressed the presence of Jews and the development of policies toward them in terms of a question. In general, social, political, and economic issues were rendered as questions: the woman question, the nationality question, not the woman problem or the nationality problem.

4   For useful overviews, see Albert Lindemann, "Introduction," in Albert Lindemann and Richard Levy, eds., *Antisemitism: A History* (Oxford: Oxford University Press, 2010), 17–33, Albert Lindemann, *Anti-semitism before the Holocaust* (New York: Longman, 2000), Jonathan Judaken, "Antisemitism and the Jewish Question," in Mitchell Hart and Tony Michels, eds., *The Cambridge History of Judaism*, volume 8 *The Modern World: 1815–2000* (Cambridge: Cambridge University Press, 2017), 559–88, David Nirenberg, *Anti-Judaism: The Western Tradition* (New York: W. W. Norton, 2013), Robert Wistrich, *A Lethal Obsession: Anti-semitism from Antiquity to the Global*

Jihad (New York: Random House, 2010), and Robert Wistrich, *Antisemitism: The Longest Hatred* (New York: Schocken, 1994).

5   The first explicit formulation of the Jewish question occurred during the 1830s in Great Britain when Parliament debated the extension of suffrage to adult Jewish males. But the status of Jews in a Europe undergoing the transition from absolute monarchies to polities based on popular sovereignty had been a topic of discussion for well over a century.

6   An extensive scholarship exists on Jewish emancipation. See David Sorkin, *Jewish Emancipation: A History Across Five Centuries* (Princeton: Princeton University Press, 2019) for a recent analysis of the process by which Jews received rights of citizenship. In addition to David Sorkin, see the classic account by Jacob Katz, *Out of the Ghetto: The Social Background of Jewish Emancipation, 1770–1870* (Cambridge, MA: Harvard University Press, 1973) and the essays in Pierre Birnbaum and Ira Katznelson, eds., *Paths of Emancipation: Jews, States, and Citizenship* (Princeton: Princeton University Press, 1995) and Jonathan Frankel and Steven Zipperstein, eds., *Assimilation and Community: The Jews in Nineteenth-Century Europe* (Cambridge: Cambridge University Press, 1992).

7   See Selected Bibliography for excellent overviews and analyses of the history of Jews in tsarist Russia.

8   To a lesser extent, Jews also lived in Siberia. Given the preponderance of Jews living in European Russia, I focus on the community of Jews living in the Pale of Settlement.

9   A thorough account is provided in John Klier, *Russia Gathers Her Jews: The Origins of the "Jewish Question" in Russia, 1772–1825* (Dekalb: Northern Illinois Press, 1986).

10 On the historiography of the Pale of Settlement, see Robert Geraci, "Pragmatism and Prejudice: Revisiting the Origin of the Pale of Jewish Settlement and Its Historiography," *Journal of Modern History* 91 (December 2019): 776–814. For a comprehensive treatment of the issue, see Klier, *Russia Gathers Her Jews: The Origins of the "Jewish Question" in Russia, 1772–1825.*

11 The data are from Alexander Orbach, "The Development of the Russian Jewish Community, 1881–1903" in John Klier and Shlomo Lambroza, eds., *Pogroms: Anti-Jewish Violence in Modern Russian History* (Cambridge: Cambridge University Press, 1992), 139.

12 For a recent history of the shtetl, see Jonathan Petrovsky-Shtern, *The Golden Age Shtetl: A New History of Jewish Life in East Europe* (Princeton: Princeton University Press, 2014).

13 Between 1880 and 1914 some two million Jews left the Russian Empire for the United States, Canada, Great Britain, and Central and Western Europe.

14 Terry Martin, *The Affirmative Action Empire: Nations and Nationalism in the Soviet Union, 1923–1939* (Ithaca: Cornell University Press, 2001) and Francine Hirsch, *Empire of Nations: Ethnographic Knowledge and the Making of the Soviet Union* (Ithaca: Cornell University Press, 2005).

15 Like the literature on Jews in tsarist Russia, many excellent studies of Soviet Jewry exist. See Selected Bibliography.

16 Quoted in Evrydiki Sifneos, *Imperial Russia: Peoples, Spaces, Identities* (Leiden: Brill, 2017), 189–90.

17 ChaeRan Freeze and Jay Harris, eds., *Everyday Jewish Life in Imperial Russia: Select Documents, 1772–1914* (Waltham, MA: Brandeis University Press, 2013), 786.

18 Shulamit Volkov, "Antisemitism as a Cultural Code: Reflections on the History and Historiography of Antisemitism in Imperial Germany," *Leo Baeck Institute Yearbook*, 23:1 (January 1978): 25–46.

19 Nirenberg, *Anti-Judaism: The Western Tradition*, 468.

20 Similar questions characterize relations between other groups. In India, for example, Hindu nationalists question the political loyalty of Muslims and question their desire to acculturate. Similarly, Muslim nationalists in Pakistan accuse Hindus of economic exploitation. I thank Nirav Mehta for pointing this out to me.

Chapter 1

1 On Zotov and Aleksandrov, see John Klier, *Imperial Russia's Jewish Question, 1855–1881*, 53 and 133.

2 Quoted in Klier, *Imperial Russia's Jewish Question, 1855–1881*, 439.

3 These comments on the Kiselev memorandum are based on Michael Stanislawski, *Tsar Nicholas I and the Jews: The Transformation of Jewish Society in Russia, 1823–1855*, 43.

4 In some instances, the children were found dead. But in many cases the children turned up alive and well soon after news of their disappearances became public.

5 For a comprehensive treatment of the blood libel in Europe prior to the nineteenth century, see Magda Teter, *Blood Libel: On the Trail of an Antisemitic Myth* (Cambridge, MA: Harvard University Press, 2020).

6 Uniates were Christians who acknowledged papal authority and Catholic doctrine but retained many Eastern Orthodox rites and rituals.

Notes

7   In the late nineteenth century a revival of ritual murder accusations also took place in Central and East Central Europe. See Hillel Kieval, *Blood Inscriptions: Science, Modernity, and Ritual Murder in Fin de Siècle Europe* (Philadelphia: University of Pennsylvania Press, 2022) and Helmut Walser Smith, *The Butcher's Tale: Murder and Anti-Semitism in a German Town* (New York: W. W. Norton, 2003).

8   In some cases non-Jews also fell victim to charges of ritual murder. For example, Old Believers (Orthodox Christians who had split from the official church in the seventeenth century) and members of small ethnic minorities sometimes found themselves the focus of investigations into murders deemed by police and prosecutors as ritually motivated.

9   Eugene Avrutin, *The Velizh Affair: Blood Libel in a Russian Town* (Oxford: Oxford University Press, 2018).

10   See the essays in Eugene Avrutin, Jonathan Dekel-Chen, and Robert Weinberg, eds., *Ritual Murder in Russia, Eastern Europe, and Beyond: New Histories of an Old Accusation* (Bloomington: Indiana University Press, 2017) and Klier, *Imperial Russia's Jewish Question*, chapter 18.

11   On the Beilis trial, see Robert Weinberg, *Blood Libel in Late Imperial Russia: The Ritual Murder Trial of Mendel Beilis* (Bloomington: Indiana University Press, 2013), Hans Rogger, "The Beilis Case: Anti-Semitism and Politics in the Reign of Nicholas II," *Slavic Review* 25: 4 (December 1966): 615–29, Edmund Levin, *A Child of Christian Blood: Murder and Conspiracy in Tsarist Russia: The Beilis Blood Libel* (New York: Schocken, 2014), and Maurice Samuel, *Blood Accusation: The Strange History of the Beiliss Case* (New York: Alfred A. Knopf, 1966).

12   For an excellent overview of the Dreyfus, Frank, and Beilis trials, see Albert Lindemann, *The Jew Accused: Three Anti-Semitic Trials (Dreyfus, Beilis, Frank), 1894–1915* (Cambridge: Cambridge University Press, 1992).

13   Hillel Kieval makes a convincing case about the blood libel as a thoroughly modern phenomenon. See Kieval, *Blood Inscriptions*.

14   Weinberg, *Blood Libel in Late Imperial Russia*, 100.

15   Mendel Beilis, *The Story of My Sufferings* (New York: Mendel Beilis, 1926), 199–200.

16   On the fate of blood libel in the first several decades of the Soviet Union, see Elissa Bemporad, *Legacy of Blood: Jews, Pogroms, and Ritual Murder in the Lands of the Soviets* (New York: Oxford University Press, 2020), especially chapter 4.

17   Anna Shternshis, *Soviet and Kosher: Jewish Popular Culture in the Soviet Union, 1923–1939* (Bloomington: Indiana University Press, 2006), 21

18   Shternshis, *Soviet and Kosher: Jewish Popular Culture in the Soviet Union, 1923–1939*, 29.

19 Nora Levin, *The Jews in the Soviet Union since 1917: The Paradox of Survival*, volume 1 (New York: New York University Press, 1988), 80.

20 Shternshis, *Soviet and Kosher: Jewish Popular Culture in the Soviet Union, 1923–1939*, 29.

21 This number—about half of the pre-1914 population of the Russian Empire—reflected the fact that two and a half million Jews now lived in newly independent Poland and Lithuania.

22 *Bezbozhnik u stanka* (The Atheist at the Work Bench) was the publication of the Moscow Society of the Godless and appeared between 1923 and 1931. Along with the journal and newspaper, both entitled *Bezhbozhnik* (The Atheist), *Bezbozhnik u stanka* played a critical role in the Kremlin's campaign against Judaism in the two decades after the revolution by providing activists with the material they needed to promote antireligious sentiment and secular values among the populace. The editors of *Bezbozhnik u stanka* used sensationalized drawings in color to attract a readership of workers. Its print-run numbered in the tens of thousands for each issue, which was subject to review by government censors.

23 Jehovah is the name of god in the Hebrew Scriptures.

24 In the Priestly Benediction, the *Kohan* (descendants of Aaron, Moses's brother, who served as priests in the Temple in Jerusalem) delivers a blessing to the congregation. Devotees of *Star Trek* will no doubt recognize the Priestly Benediction as the Vulcan hand greeting ("Live Long and Prosper") used by Mr. Spock played by Leonard Nimoy. Nimoy said that he remembered the gesture from services in the synagogue he attended as a youth.

25 Phylacteries (*Tefillin* in Hebrew) are two small, leather cases containing pieces of paper with passages from the Hebrew Scriptures. During the morning prayer a male Jew fastens one phylactery with leather strips to the forehead and another one to the left arm.

26 W. F. Ryan, *The Bathhouse at Midnight: An Historical Survey of Magic and Divination in Russia* (University Park: Pennsylvania State University Press, 1999), 32–4.

27 Lesley Brown, ed., *The New Shorter Oxford English Dictionary on Historical Principles*, volume 2 (Oxford: Clarendon Press, 1993), 2870.

28 Victoria Bonnell, *Iconography of Power: Soviet Political Posters under Lenin and Stalin* (Berkeley: University of California Press, 1999), 42 and 159 and Boris Uspensky, *The Semiotics of the Russian Icon*, edited by Stephen Rudy (Lisse, Belgium: Peter de Ridder Press, 1976), 39.

29 See Douglas Smith, *Working the Rough Stone: Freemasonry and Society in Eighteenth-Century Russia* (Dekalb: Northern Illinois University Press, 1999).

Notes

30   The Eye of Providence was also associated with other secret groups such as the Illuminati who opposed what they considered to be superstition, undue religious influence, and abuses of power by governments. Church and state officials accused them of being a cabal intent on dominating the world.

31   Alan M. Ball, *Russia's Last Capitalists: The Nepmen, 1921–1929* (Berkeley: University of California Press, 1987), 165.

32   Iris Idelson-Shein, "Introduction: Writing a History of Horror, or What Happens When Monsters Stare Back," in Iris Idelson-Shein and Christian Wiese, eds. *Monsters and Monstrosity in Jewish History: From the Middle Ages to Modernity* (London: Bloomsbury Academic, 2010), 1.

33   Babyn Yar was a ravine on the outskirts of Kyiv where German troops murdered some 33,000 Jews during the initial days of Germany's occupation of Ukraine's capital in September 1941. Over the next several years, an additional 70,000 Jews and non-Jews were shot at the ravine.

34   Benjamin Pinkus, *The Jews of the Soviet Union: The History of a National Minority* (Cambridge: Cambridge University Press, 1988), 207–8.

35   Zvi Gitelman, *A Century of Ambivalence: The Jews of Russia and the Soviet Union, 1881 to the Present*, 2nd edition (Bloomington: Indiana University Press, 2001), 164.

36   See Chapter 4 for a discussion of the *Protocols*.

37   See Moshe Decter, "'Judaism without Embellishment': Recent Documentation of Russian Anti-Semitism." Reprint from *New Politics: A Quarterly Journal of Socialist Thought* (1963): 105–7.

Chapter 2

1   The Edict of Tolerance (January 2, 1782) in Paul Mendes-Flohr and Jehuda Reinharz, eds., *The Jew in the Modern World: A Documentary History*, 3rd edition (New York: Oxford University Press, 2011), 42–5.

2   Berr Isaac Berr, "Letter of a Citizen to His Fellow Jews (1791)," in Paul Mendes-Flohr and Jehuda Reinharz, eds., *The Jew in the Modern World: A Documentary History*, 3rd edition (New York: Oxford University Press, 2011), 128–30.

3   On the Jewish Enlightenment in Central Europe, see Michael Meyer, *The Origins of the Modern Jew: Jewish Identity and European Culture in Germany, 1749*-1824 (Detroit, MI: Wayne State University Press, 1967), David Sorkin, *The Transformation of German Jewry, 1780-1840* (Oxford: Oxford University Press, 1987), and David Sorkin, *Moses*

Mendelsohn and the Religious Enlightenment (Berkeley: University of California Press, 1996).

4 For a discussion of "selective integration," see Benjamin Nathans, *Beyond the Pale: The Jewish Encounter with Late Imperial Russia* (Berkeley: University of California Press, 2004).

5 On Jews in the tsarist military, see Olga Litvak, *Conscription and the Search for Modern Jewry* (Bloomington: Indiana University Press, 2006), Jonathan Petrovsky-Shtern, *Jews in the Russian Army, 1827-1917: Drafted into Modernity* (Cambridge: Cambridge University Press, 2009), and Stanislawski, *Tsar Nicholas I and the Jews: The Transformation of Jewish Society in Russia, 1825-1855*.

6 Stanislawski, *Tsar Nicholas I and the Jews: The Transformation of Jewish Society in Russia, 1825-1855*, 22–5.

7 Stanislawski, *Tsar Nicholas I and the Jews: The Transformation of Jewish Society in Russia, 1825-1855*, 30.

8 Jarrod Tanny, "The Jews in the Land of the Russian Tsars," in Alan T. Levenson, ed., *The Wiley-Blackwell History of Jews and Judaism* (Malden, MA: Blackwell, 2012), 369. Michael Stanislawski was the first to make this argument in *Tsar Nicholas I and the Jews*.

9 On the education of Jewish girls, see Eliyana Adler, *In Her Hands: The Education of Jewish Girls in Tsarist Russia* (Detroit, MI: Wayne State University Press, 2011) and Carole Bailin, *To Reveal Our Hearts: Jewish Women Writers in Tsarist Russia* (Cincinnati, OH: Hebrew Union College Press, 2000).

10 Freeze and Harris, *Everyday Jewish Life in Imperial Russia: Select Documents, 1772-1914*, 63.

11 Stanislawski, *Tsar Nicholas I and the Jews: The Transformation of Jewish Society in Russia, 1825-1855*, 83.

12 The peasant emancipation, in conjunction with the development of the railway system, weakened the role played by Jews in the marketing of grain and limited the supply of manufactured goods available outside urban areas. In addition, the government's decision in the mid-1890s to impose a monopoly on the sale of vodka made matters worse since it meant that Jewish tavernkeepers lost a significant source of income. By the eve of the First World War the monopoly provided one-third of the government's budget.

13 Nathans, *Beyond the Pale: The Jewish Encounter with Late Imperial Russia*, 270–1.

14 See the memoirs of Pauline Wengeroff, which offer insights into the clash between traditional Jewish society and the challenges of the secular world. *Memoirs of a Grandmother: Scenes from the Cultural History of*

Notes

Jews Russia in the Nineteenth Century. 2 volumes (Stanford: Stanford University Press, 2010 and 2020).

15   Zipperstein, *The Jews of Odessa: A Cultural History, 1794-1881.*

16   Ellie Schainker, *Confessions of the Shtetl: Converts from Judaism in Imperial Russia, 1817-1906* (Stanford: Stanford University Press, 2016). See also ChaeRan Freeze, *Jewish Marriage and Divorce in Imperial Russia* (Hanover, NH: University Press of New England, 2002).

17   Freeze and Harris, *Everday Jewish Life in Imperial Russia: Select Documents, 1772-1914*, 268–9.

18   Zvi Gitelman, *A Century of Ambivalence: The Jews of Russia and the Soviet Union, 1881 to the Present*, 2nd edition (Bloomington: Indiana University Press, 2001), 111.

19   Viacheslav Konstantinov, *Evreiskoe naselenia byvshego SSSR v XX veke* (Jerusalem: Izdatel'stvo LIRA, 2007), 28–30, 39–40, 69. These figures on marriages pertain to Russia, Ukraine, and Belarus.

20   Jeffrey Veidlinger, *The Moscow State Yiddish Theater: Jewish Culture on the Soviet Stage* (Bloomington: Indiana University Press, 2000).

21   See Slezkine, *The Jewish Century*, 239 and 277.

22   Shternshis, *Soviet and Kosher: Jewish Popular Culture in the Soviet Union, 1923-1917.* See also her *When Sonia Met Boris: An Oral History of Jewish Life under Stalin* (New York: Oxford University Press, 2017).

23   Zvi Gitelman, "The Meanings of Jewishness in Post-Soviet Russia and Ukraine," in Eliezer Ben Rafael, Yosef Gorni, and Yaacov Ro'i, eds., *Contemporary Jewries: Convergence and Divergence* (Leiden: Brill, 2003), 196.

Chapter 3

1   Derek J. Penslar, *Shylock's Children: Economics and Jewish Identity in Modern Europe* (Berkeley: University of California Press, 2001), 53.

2   Laurie Bernstein, *Sonia's Daughters: Prostitutes and Their Regulation in Imperial Russia* (Berkeley: University of California Press, 1995), 164.

3   Quoted in Hans Rogger, "Government, Jews, Peasants, and Land in Post-Emancipation Russia," *Cahiers du Monde Russe*, 17: 2/3 (1976): 173.

4   Fyodor Dostoevsky, "The Jewish Question," in *A Writer's Diary*, translated and annotated by Kenneth Lantz, volume 2 (Evanston, IL: Northwestern University Press, 1993), 907 and 913–15.

5   Those deprived of electoral rights were known as *lishentsy*.

6   Viacheslav Konstantinov, *Evreiskoe naselenie byvshego SSSR v XX veke (sotsial'no-demografcheskii analiz)* (Jerusalem: Izdatel'stvo LIRA, 2007), 164–6.

7   Zionism was a political and intellectual movement that emerged in the late nineteenth century and advocated for the establishment of an independent Jewish state.

8   For an excellent discussion of Jewish agricultural colonies in the 1920s and 1930s, particularly in the Crimea, see Jonathan Dekel-Chen, *Farming the Red Land: Jewish Agricultural Colonization and Local Soviet Power, 1924-1941* (New Haven, CT: Yale University Press, 2005).

9   For a discussion of literary treatments of Jewish pig breading in Birobidzhan, see Gennady Estraikh, "Pig-Breeding, Shiksas, and Other Goyish Themes in Soviet Yiddish Literature and Life," *Symposium: A Quarterly Journal in Modern Literatures*, 57: 3 (2003): 161–4.

10 A recent history of Birobidzhan is given in Gennady Estraikh, *The History of Birobidzhan: Building a Soviet Jewish Homeland in Siberia* (London: Bloomsbury, 2023). See also Robert Weinberg, *Stalin's Forgotten Zion: Birobidzhan and the Making of a Soviet Jewish Homeland. An Illustrated History, 1928-1996* (Berkeley: University of California Press, 1998).

11 Quoted in Zvi Gitelman, *Jewish Nationality and Soviet Politics: The Jewish Sections of the CPSU, 1917-1930* (Princeton: Princeton University Press, 1972), 416–17.

12 *Tribuna evreiskoi sovetskoi obshchestvennosti*, October 1, 1928, 1.

13 For these quotations, see, respectively, A. Fabrikant, "Agrikul'turnye cherty evreiskogo zemledeliia v SSSR," *Evreiskii krest'ianin*, no. 1 (1925): 24, *Tribuna evreiskoi sovetskoi obshchestvennosti* (September 1, 1928): 21, and State Archive of the Jewish Autonomous Region, *fond* 3, *opis'* 1, *delo* 13, *listy* 2 and 4–5.

14 Mary Leder, *My Life in Stalinist Russia: An American Woman Looks Back* (Bloomington: Indiana University Press, 2002), 15–25. Mary Leder was an American teenager whose parents relocated to Birobidzhan from Los Angeles in the early 1930s. She left for Moscow due to the difficult living conditions on a collective farm in Birobidzhan.

15 Benjamin Pinkus, *The Soviet Government and the Jews: A Documented Study* (Cambridge: Cambridge University Press, 1984), 62–3.

Chapter 4

1   Erich Haberer, *Jews and Revolution in Nineteenth-Century Russia* (Cambridge: Cambridge University Press, 1995), 253.

2   Barbara Alpern Engel, "Gesia Gelfman: A Jewish Woman on the Left in Imperial Russia," in Jack Jacobs, ed, *Judaism and Leftist Politics: Judaism,*

Notes

Israel, Antisemitism, and Gender (New York: Cambridge University Press, 2017), 183 and 198.

3   The best treatment of Jewish radicalism remains. See Jonathan Frankel, *Prophecy and Politics: Socialism, Nationalism, and the Russian Jews, 1862-1917* (Cambridge: Cambridge University Press, 1981). See also Ezra Mendelsohn, *Class Struggle in the Pale: The Formative Years of the Jewish Workers' Movement in Tsarist Russia* (Cambridge: Cambridge University Press, 1970).

4   The best treatment of the 1905 revolution is Abraham Ascher, *The Revolution of 1905.* 2 volumes (Stanford: Stanford University Press, 1988 and 1992).

5   The first Russian-language translation of Bram Stoker's novel *Dracula* appeared in 1902.

6   John Klier, *Russians, Jews, and the Pogroms of 1881-1882* (Cambridge: Cambridge University Press, 2011). On the Kishinev pogrom, see Steven Zipperstein, *Pogrom: Kishinev and the Tilt of History* (New York: W. W. Norton, 2018) and Edward Judge, *Easter in Kishinev: Anatomy of a Pogrom* (New York: New York University Press, 1992).

7   Elissa Bemporad, *Legacy of Blood: Jews, Pogroms, and Ritual Murder in the Land of the Soviets* (New York: Oxford University Press, 2019), 22.

8   The following books provide excellent overviews of the pogroms: Irina Astashkevich, *Gendered Violence: Jewish Women in the Pogroms of 1917 to 1921* (Boston: Academic Studies Press, 2018) and Jeffrey Veidlinger, *In the Midst of Civilized Europe: The Pogroms of 1918-1921 and the Onset of the Holocaust* (New York: Metropolitan Books, 2021). See also some of the essays in Eugene Avrutin and Elissa Bemporad, eds., *Pogroms: A Documentary History* (New York: Oxford University Press, 2021), Jonathan Dekel-Chen, ed., *Anti-Jewish Violence: Rethinking the Pogrom in Eastern Europe* (Bloomington: Indiana University Press, 2010), and John Klier and Shlomo Lambroza, eds., *Pogroms: Anti-Jewish Violence in Modern Russian History* (New York: Cambridge University Press, 1992).

9   This discussion of Brafman is based on Klier, *Imperial Russia's Jewish Question, 1855-1881*, 263–74.

10   Klier, *Imperial Russia's Jewish Question, 1855-1881*, 272.

11   Krushevan may have been assisted by someone else in writing the book.

12   Zipperstein, *Pogrom: Kishinev and the Tilt of History*, 159--64.

13   "Protocols of the Elders of Zion," in Paul Mendes-Flohr and Jehuda Reinharz, eds., *The Jew in the Modern World: A Documentary History.* Third Edition (New York: Oxford University Press, 2011), 340.

14   See Oleg Budnitskii, *Russian Jews between the Reds and the Whites, 1917-1920* (Philadelphia: University of Pennsylvania Press, 2012).

15   Brendan McGeever, "The Bolsheviks and Antisemitism," *Jacobin*, June 22, 2017. See also his *Antisemitism and the Russian Revolution* (Cambridge: Cambridge University Press, 2019).

16   "Building socialism" refers to the Kremlin's effort to create an industrialized and urbanized country. It entailed state-ownership of agriculture, industry and commerce, a planned economy, and an equitable, classless society rooted in a collectivist ethos.

17   Slezkine, *The Jewish Century*, 180.

18   For books about the fate of Soviet Jews in the period immediately after the Second World War, see Gennady Kostyrchenko, *Out of the Red Shadows: Anti-Semitism in Stalin's Russia* (Amherst, MA: Prometheus Books, 1995), Shimon Redlich, *War, Holocaust, and Stalinism: A Documented Study of the Jewish Anti-Fascist Committee* (Luxembourg: Harwood Academic Publishers, 1995), Joshua Rubenstein and Vladimir Naumov, eds., *Stalin's Secret Pogrom: The Postwar Inquisition of the Jewish Anti-Fascist Committee* (New Haven, CT: Yale University Press, 2001), and Yehoshua Gilboa, *The Black Years of Soviet Jewry, 1939-*1953 (Boston: Little, Brown, 1971.

19   The government arrested fifteen Jews, but one fell into a coma and died several months after the execution of the others. He was not put on trial.

20   Rubenstein and Naumov, *Stalin's Secret Pogrom: The Postwar Inquisition of the Jewish Antifascist Committee*, 1–64.

21   "Spies and Murderers in the Guise of Physicians and Scientists," *Izvestiia* (January 13, 1953). The faulty logic of accusing Soviet Jews of being both cosmopolitan or internationalist citizens of the world and nationalists loyal to the State of Israel at the same time evidently did not bother the architects of the Soviet Union's Jewish policy who believed that Jewish nationalism and cosmopolitanism could coexist.

22   Levin, *The Jews in the Soviet Union since 1917: Paradox of Survival*, volume 2, 543.

23   Anna Shternshis, *When Sonia Met Boris: An Oral History of Jewish Life under Stalin* (New York: Oxford University Press, 2017), 153.

24   Alexander Lokshin, "The Doctors' Plot: The Non-Jewish Response," in Yaacov Ro'i, ed., *Jews and Jewish Life in Russia and the Soviet Union* (Portland, OR: Frank Cass, 1995), 157.

25   Zvi Gitelman, *Jewish Identities in Postcommunist Russia and Ukraine: An Uncertain Ethnicity* (Cambrdige: Cambridge University Press, 2012), 185.

26   Gitelman, *Jewish Identities in Postcommunist Russia and Ukraine: An Uncertain Ethnicity*, 184–5.

Epilogue

1   On the other hand, Putin's minister of foreign affairs Sergei Lavrov claimed, soon after Russia invaded Ukraine in 2022, that Zelensky supported neo-Nazis in Ukraine. Lavrov also repeated the discredited view that Hitler had a Jewish grandfather.

2   Mark Tolts, "A Half Century of Jewish Emigration from the Former Soviet Union: Demographic Aspects." Paper presented to the Davis Center, Harvard University, on November 20, 2019.

3   Gitelman, *Jewish Identities in Postcommunist Russia and Ukraine: An Uncertain*, chapter 8.

4   Georgii Gorodentsev, "Pussy Riot i M. Beilis: Koshchunstvo v Khrame Khrista Spasitelia: Prestuplenie i Nakazanie," *Russkaia narodnaia liniia* (March 21, 2012), 1 and Aleksandr Shumskii, "'Pusi Raiot'—Novoe delo Beilisa: Koshchunstvo v Khrame Khrista Spasitelia: Prestuplenie i Nakazanie," *Russkaia narodnaia liniia* (June 28, 2012), 1–2,

5   "Lawyers of the Victims: Pussy Riot Led by Satan." https://www.bbc.com/russian/rolling_news/2012/07/120719_rn_pussy_riot_trial. Accessed January 20, 2023.

SELECTED BIBLIOGRAPHY

Aronson, I. Michael. *Troubled Waters: Origins of the 1881 Anti-Jewish Pogroms in Russia.* Pittsburgh: University of Pittsburgh Press, 1990.

Avrutin, Eugene. *The Jews and the Imperial State: Identification Politics in Tsarist Russia.* Ithaca, NY: Cornell University Press. 2010.

Avrutin, Eugene. *The Velizh Affair: Blood Libel in a Russian Town.* Oxford: Oxford University Press, 2017.

Bemoporad, Elissa. *Becoming Soviet Jews: The Bolshevik Experiment in Minsk.* Bloomington: Indiana University Press, 2013.

Bemporad, Elissa. *Legacy of Blood: Jews, Pogroms, and Ritual Murder in the Land of the Soviets.* New York: Oxford University Press, 2019.

Budnitskii, Oleg. *Russian Jews between the Reds and the Whites, 1917–1920.* Philadelphia: University of Pennsylvania Press, 2012.

Dekel-Chen, Jonathan. *Farming the Red Land: Agricultural Colonization and Local Soviet Power, 1924–1941.* New Haven, CT: Yale University Press, 2008.

Frankel, Jonathan. *Prophecy and Politics: Socialism, Nationalism, and the Russian Jews, 1862–1917.* Cambridge: Cambridge University Press, 1981.

Freeze, ChaeRan and Harris, Jay Michael, eds., *Everyday Jewish Life in Imperial Russia Selected Documents, 1772–1914.* Waltham, MA: Brandeis University Press, 2013,

Gitelman, Zvi. *A Century of Ambivalence: The Jews of Russia and the Soviet Union, 1881 to the Present.* Second edition. Bloomington: Indiana University Press, 2001.

Gitelman, Zvi. *Jewish Identities in Postcommunist Russia and Ukraine: An Uncertain Ethnicity.* Cambridge: Cambridge University Press, 2012.

Gitelman, Zvi. *Jewish Nationality Policy and Soviet Politics: The Jewish Sections of the CPSU, 1917–1930.* Princeton: Princeton University Press, 1972.

Horowitz, Brian. *Empire Jews: Jewish Nationalism and Acculturation in 19th- and Early 20th-Century Russia.* Bloomington, IN: Slavica Publishers, 2009.

Klier, John. *Imperial Russia's Jewish Question, 1855–1881.* Cambridge: Cambridge University Press, 1995.

Selected Bibliography

Klier, John. *Russia Gathers Her Jews: The Origins of the "Jewish Question" in Russia, 1772–1825*. DeKalb: Northern Illinois Press. 1986.

Klier, John. *Russians, Jews, and the Pogroms of 1881–1882*. Cambridge: Cambridge University Press, 2011.

Lederhendler, Eli. *The Road to Modern Jewish Politics: Political Tradition and Political Reconstruction in the Jewish Community of Tsarist Russia*. Oxford: Oxford University Press, 1989.

Levin, Nora. *The Jews in the Soviet Union since 1917*. 2 vols. London: I. B. Tauris, 1988.

Litvak, Olga, *Conscription and the Search for Modern Jewry*. Bloomington: Indiana University Press, 2006.

Löwe, Heinz-Dietrich. *The Tsars and the Jews: Reform, Reaction, and Anti-Semitism in Imperial Russia, 1772–1917*. New York: Harwood Academic Publishers, 1993.

Meir, Natan. *Kiev, Jewish Metropolis: A History, 1859–1914*. Bloomington: Indiana University Press, 2010.

Nathans, Benjamin. *Beyond the Pale: The Jewish Encounter with Late Imperial Russia*. Berkeley: University of California Press, 2002.

Petrovsky-Shtern, Jonathan. *Jews in the Russian Army, 1827–1917: Drafted into Modernity*. Cambridge: Cambridge University Press, 2009.

Petrovsky-Shtern, Jonathan. *The Golden Age Shtetl: A New History of Jewish Life in East Europe*. Princeton: Princeton University Press, 2014.

Pinkus, Benjamin. *The Jews of the Soviet Union: The History of a National Minority*. Cambridge: Cambridge University Press, 1988.

Ro'i, Yaacov, ed., *Jews and Jewish Life in Russia and the Soviet Union*. Portland, OR: Frank Cass, 1995.

Rubenstein, Joshua, and Naumov, Vladimir, eds. *Stalin's Secret Pogrom: The Postwar Inquisition of the Jewish Antifascist Committee*. New Haven, CT: Yale University Press. 2001.

Shneer, David. *Yiddish and the Creation of Soviet Jewish Culture, 1918–1930*. Cambridge: Cambridge University Press, 2004.

Shternshis, Anna. *Soviet and Kosher: Jewish Popular Culture in the Soviet Union, 1923–1939*. Bloomington: Indiana University Press, 2006.

Shternshis, Anna. *When Sonia Met Boris: An Oral History of Jewish Life Under Stalin*. Oxford: Oxford University Press, 2017.

Slezkine, Yuri. *The Jewish Century*. Princeton: Princeton University Press, 2004.

Stanislawski, Michael. *Tsar Nicholas I and the Jews: The Transformation of Jewish Society in Russia, 1825–1855*. Philadelphia: Jewish Publication Society of America. 1983.

Tanny, Jarrod. *City of Rogues and Schnorrers: Russia's Jews and the Myth of Old Odessa*. Bloomington: Indiana University Press, 2011.

Veidlinger, Jeffrey. *In the Midst of Civilized Europe: The Pogroms of 1918–1921 and the Onset of the Holocaust*. New York: Metropolitan Books. 2021.

Veidlinger, Jeffrey. *Jewish Public Culture in the Late Russian Empire*. Bloomington: Indiana University Press. 2009. 94–188.

Weinberg, Robert. *Ritual Murder in Late Imperial Russia: The Ritual Murder Trial of Mendel Beilis*. Bloomington: Indiana University Press, 2013.

Weinberg, Robert. *Stalin's Forgotten Zion: Birobidzhan and the Making of a Soviet Jewish History: An Illustrated History, 1928–1996*. Berkeley: University of California Press, 1998.

Zipperstein, Steven. *The Jews of Odessa: A Cultural History, 1794–1881*. Stanford: Stanford University Press, 1985.

Zipperstein, Steven. *Pogrom: Kishinev and the Tilt of History*. New York: W. W. Norton, 2018.

INDEX

Index

Index

Index